Cultivating Sherlock Holmes

Cultivating Sherlock Holmes

Edited by
Bryce L. Crawford, Jr.
and
Joseph B. Connors

"IS THERE ANY OTHER POINT WHICH I CAN MAKE CLEAR?"

Published by the Sumac Press, La Crosse, Wisconsin

for the Norwegian Explorers of Minnesota

1473 Fulham Street, St. Paul, 55108

1978

DEDICATED TO THE MEMORY OF:

Theodore C. Blegen, 1891-1969
Thomas L. Daniels, B.S.I. 1892-1977
Philip S. Hench, 1896-1965

———————————

"Stand with me here upon the terrace..."

Contents

CULTIVATING SHERLOCK HOLMES

Introduction
Bryce L. Crawford, Jr.

THE YEAR 1978 holds a special timeliness for the publication of a fourth volume by the Norwegian Explorers of Minnesota, setting forth observations and interpretations regarding the career of Sherlock Holmes. And we bring forth this volume with a particular sense of the time being appropriate. For the year marks, in the first place, the 100th anniversary of the beginning of Mr. Holmes's professional practice; the details have been recorded and worked out in too many volumes of Baker Street studies for us to extend comments here. And at the same time, 1978 marks the 30th anniversary of the formation, or at least the first formal meeting, of the Norwegian Explorers.

It is of course a bit difficult to be absolutely certain of the precise date for either of these beginnings. It is suitably recorded and well defined that the first actual meeting, with prior announcements and a certain formality, was held on January 23, 1948, when some seven Sherlockian students came together at the Covered Wagon in Minneapolis to initiate this new scion society, one of several, the appropriate notice being sent out by E. W. McDiarmid as Sigerson of the newly formed group.

But the preliminaries of that first formal meeting are a little harder to track down definitively. We can say with confidence that, some time about the middle of 1947, a half dozen Sherlockian devotees at the University of Minnesota came together in the Campus Club to discuss the possibility of forming a scion society. Blegen the Historian and Graduate Dean, Armstrong of Physiological Chemistry, Crawford of Chemistry, McDiarmid of the University Library, and Ziebarth of Speech and Theater Arts came to the agreement that this would be a good enterprise to start. There is a record of the discussion and some further correspondence, with McDiarmid signing as "Gasogene" of the Norwegian Explorers. It is of course obvious that in Minnesota a group of Sherlockians could well call themselves the Norwegian Explorers, in honor of the original use in the Canon of the name Sigerson[1]; and it is not inap-

---

1. "You may have read of the remarkable explorations of a Norwegian named Sigerson, but I am sure that it never occurred to you that you were receiving news of your friend." From the "Adventure of the Empty House."

propriate that this recognition of the name carried it forward to its institution as a title or a designation of responsibility.

Bryce L.
Crawford Jr.

The earlier use of the term "Gasogene" also is a clear indication that, right from the start, this group of Sherlockians intended to join with the numerous scion societies then forming all over the country, affiliating with the original American group, the Baker Street Irregulars of New York, who originated the term "Gasogene" in their early meetings in the mid-30's. Right on through the 30 years of activity on the part of the Norwegian Explorers, appropriate contact has been maintained with this central New York group, and indeed a number of the Norwegian Explorers have also been appropriately invested as members of the Baker Street Irregulars, and are thus entitled to append the initials "B.S.I." in their correspondence. From time to time, in the same way, the Norwegian Explorers have been represented at the annual January dinner in New York, commemorating the birthday of Mr. Holmes, which the Baker Street Irregulars hold each year.

Throughout the years the Norwegian Explorers, like other scion societies, have carried on such activities as discussions (sometimes even arguments), viewing and criticism of motion picture films and the like, and particularly the publication either as individuals or as a society, of scholarly contributions to the literature on Sherlock Holmes. The first publication from the Norwegian Explorers appeared in 1951, containing *The Crowded Box Room,* a study of Holmes's imagery by T. C. Blegen. This volume was followed a year later by a second publication from the Explorers, *Sherlock Holmes: Master Detective* containing half a dozen essays commenting on Sherlock Holmes and his adventures and his character, contributed by various members of the Norwegian Explorers.

These two successful publications gave stimulus to a wider ambition on the part of the Norwegian Explorers; and while it is again difficult to date precisely the first discussions of the major project which was next undertaken, it is clear that by 1955 at the latest the group was actively moving forward to explore the possibility of marking with an appropriate plaque the location at the Reichenbach Falls where Mr. Holmes and Professor Moriarty had their final confrontation. It would appear that the project had its origin in the mind of Dr. Philip S. Hench, who brought to Sherlockian studies the same thoroughness and enthusiasm which, applied to other fields such as cortisone therapy, brought him the Nobel Prize. Certain it is that Dr. Hench was outraged to find that there was no appropriate marker at the Reichenbach Falls, and indeed that the precise location of the struggle had not been adequately studied. He himself, and later other members of the Norwegian Explorers, took up this question as an appropriate one for the Norwegian Explorers to resolve. And so it came to pass that in mid-1957, a small group of representatives of the Norwegian Explorers first visited London to meet with the Sherlock Holmes Society of London, who co-sponsored the plaque, then proceeded to the town of Meiringen where, on the rainy day of June 25, 1957, the plaque was duly installed at an appropriate spot, indicating with some precision the actual location of the epic struggle.[2]

This achievement, with appropriate details concerning the plaque, were described and presented in the third publication, *Exploring Sherlock Holmes,* appearing in 1957, and including four or five essays having to do with other aspects of the Holmesian Canon as well as the Meiringen site.

In addition to these typical contributions to Sherlockian studies, the Norwegian Explorers have always sought to introduce other individuals to this pure form of scholarship. In 1974, through the efforts of the Norwegian Explorers and other friends, a fine collection on Sherlock Holmes was purchased and installed in the University of Minnesota Libraries, forming the first nucleus of a substantial Sherlock Holmes collection. Again in 1977, the Norwegian Explorers supported an honors colloquium for liberal arts students in the University of Minnesota, under the mentorship of Andrew Malec of the Norwegian Explorers.

And somewhat in this spirit of stimulating familiarity with Sherlock Holmes among a wider group of individuals, the Norwegian Explorers took pleasure in presenting, in November of 1975, a public lecture on "The Cult of Sherlock Holmes" by John Bennett Shaw, B.S.I., the noted Sherlockian of Santa Fe, New Mexico, and the founder of the scion society, the Brothers Three of Moriarty, New Mexico. Attendance at this lecture was gratifying, and bore witness to the validity of the point made in Mr. Shaw's presentation, that more and more laymen were being attracted to the study of the Sherlockian Canon, and that indeed there was a new awakening of gen-

2. "Across this 'dreadful cauldron' occurred the culminating event in the career of Sherlock Holmes, the world's greatest detective, when on May 4, 1891, he vanquished Prof. Moriarty the Napoleon of Crime"

eral interest and of Sherlockian scholarship throughout the land. There was, and is continuing, a flow of new books, new plays, new motion pictures, all based on the life and activities of Sherlock Holmes and Dr. Watson. And it seemed to the Norwegian Explorers that it would be appropriate to invite yet others to join the "Cult of Sherlock Holmes" as Mr. Shaw refers to it, and define for themselves the keen, refreshing pleasure of cultivating this field of scholarship. So in this year we bring forth this fourth publication, including Mr. Shaw's lecture and certain other studies contributed by members of the Norwegian Explorers, once more presented with the superb craftsmanship of the Norwegian Explorers' constant friend and distinguished printer, Emerson G. Wulling of the Sumac Press.

To the seasoned Sherlockian scholar we hope these contributions will be welcome and refreshing, even perhaps in one or two points stimulating as controversial scholarship should be. To the layman who has not yet become acquainted with Sherlock Holmes, we hope that this volume, beginning with Mr. Shaw's superb presentation and continuing with a few illustrations of the joyousness of Sherlockian scholarship, may prove stimulating in a friendlier sense. So we invite the reader, whether for the first or hundredth time, to dip into the Canon and "refresh himself in a romantic chamber of the heart: in a nostalgic country of the mind: where it is always 1895."

9

Bryce L.
Crawford Jr.

EDITOR'S NOTE: *It will be obvious to the discriminating reader that Mr. Shaw's "essay" was not prepared as an article to be published but to be delivered as a lecture. And indeed, this is exactly what occurred in Minneapolis, Minnesota, on the afternoon of Thursday, November 13, 1975. Sponsored by the University of Minnesota's Departments of English, Humanities, and Concerts and Lectures in cooperation with The Norwegian Explorers, Mr. Shaw spoke to an enthusiastic audience of Explorers and friends. Mr. Shaw's lecture was recorded and a draft typed from the recording. After several modifications where the tape was faulty, the copy was submitted to Mr. Shaw for corrections, which have been incorporated into the following essay. Both we and Mr. Shaw hope that readers will realize the difficulty of transferring an oral presentation into a written piece and make allowances accordingly for the fact that we cannot adequately display in this "cold print" Mr. Shaw's charming presence, his witty manner, and the delightful rapport which existed between him and his audience.*

THE CULT OF SHERLOCK HOLMES
John Bennett Shaw, B.S.I.

FIRST, I'm going to talk seriously and shortly about three men involved in this whole subject. One is Sherlock Holmes, probably William Sherlock Holmes. He was born on January 6, 1854, in the North Riding of Yorkshire. A few scholars, particularly Franklin Roosevelt, have argued that he was born in this country. Although F.D.R. was usually right, in this case I'm sure he wasn't—even though he did write a series of letters trying to prove his point.

Sherlock's father, a country squire, was probably named Sigerson, a name which shows a Scandinavian ancestry, not uncommon here in the land of the Norwegian Explorers. His maternal grandmother was a sister of Horace Vernet, the French painter. That's why Holmes once said, "Art in the blood is liable to take the strangest forms." He had two brothers, Mycroft and Sherrinford. Mycroft, who was born in 1846 or 1847, lived quietly across from the Diogenes Club and worked for the government (Holmes said that at times Mycroft *was* the government). Of the other brother we know nothing. It has been suggested that he came to this country, went west, and hasn't been heard from since.

It's a much debated point as to whether Sherlock attended Cambridge or Oxford. Two of the great Holmesian scholars, Dorothy Sayers and Ronald Knox, argued this question for years. It's not settled.[1] We know he didn't stay for his degree. He came down to London after about two years.

Watson's first description of Holmes in *A Study in Scarlet* is a description that lingers. William Gillette, the great American actor, modeled himself on it, though he did add the calabash pipe, supposedly because the regular pipe obscured his handsome profile. Holmes did not smoke a calabash.

> His very person and appearance were such as to strike the attention of the most casual observer. In height he was rather over six feet, and so excessively lean that he seemed to be considerably taller. His eyes were sharp and piercing...and his thin, hawk-like nose gave his whole expression an air of alertness and decision. His chin, too, had the prominence and squareness which mark the man of determination.

1. We believe Mr. Connors has settled it. See his essay "Holmes and the Oxford Manner." –Ed.

John Bennett
Shaw, B.S.I.

Many things about Holmes have intrigued his biographers; for example, his defeat at the hands of Irene Adler. The facts that he never looked at another woman after Irene and that he always referred to her as *the* woman" indicated that the defeat was more general than Holmes suspected. We do know that he said he was the world's first consulting detective and that he practiced from 1879 or 1880 to October 1903, when he retired to keep bees as he is still doing in Sussex. He did come out of retirement in World War I for an assignment that took two years. He went to Chicago, assumed the identity of an Irish revolutionary named Altamont, and finally trapped Von Bork, the German spy.

Of Holmes, G. K. Chesterton said, "He is the only real legend of our time." During World War I, when Marshal Foch was commander of the French army of the Allies, Sir Arthur Conan Doyle visited the front. The Marshal said that he was shocked that Holmes was not at the front, and Doyle hastened to explain that he was probably there in disguise.

J. B. Priestley once referred to Holmes as "the stately Holmes of England." He is a world figure. Believe it or not, he is still receiving an average of ten letters a week, which are actually answered (in a rather cursory way) by a person who works for the Abbey National Building Society, which is more or less on the site where 221B would have been.

Colorado State University gave Holmes an honorary diploma, citing his various accomplishments, among them marksmanship. Also cited was the fact that he has contributed considerably to the English language, both in his style of speech and in his memorable statements on a variety of subjects.

On the subject of detection and crime, for example:

> "It is a capital mistake to theorize before one has data. Insensibly, one begins to twist facts to suit theories, instead of theories to suit facts."

> "They say that genius is an infinite capacity for taking pains. It's a very bad definition, but it does apply to detective work."

> "...when a fact appears to be opposed to a long train of deductions, it invariably proves to be capable of bearing some other interpretation."

"There's the scarlet thread of murder running through the colourless skein of life, and our duty is to unravel it, and isolate it, and expose every inch of it."

John Bennett
Shaw, B.S.I.

On women:

"I assure you that the most winning woman I ever knew was hanged for poisoning three little children for their insurance-money."

"Women are never to be entirely trusted—not the best of them."

"But love is an emotional thing, and whatever is emotional is opposed to that true cold reason which I place above all things. I should never marry myself, lest I bias my judgment."

On himself:

"I think I may go so far as to say, Watson, that I have not lived wholly in vain. If my record were closed tonight I could still survey it with equanimity. The air of London is the sweeter for my presence. In over a thousand cases I am not aware that I have ever used my powers upon the wrong side."

His two most famous remarks are to be found in "Silver Blaze" and "The Adventure of the Devil's Foot," respectively:

"Is there any other point to which you would wish to draw my attention?"
Holmes: "To the curious incident of the dog in the night-time."
Gregory: "The dog did nothing in the night-time."
Holmes: "That was the curious incident."

Sterndale: "How do you know that?"
Holmes: "I followed you."
Sterndale: "I saw no one."
Holmes: "That is what you may expect to see when I follow you."

John Bennett
Shaw, B.S.I.

A second man to mention briefly is John H. Watson, whose middle name was either Henry or Hamish. The reason for considering Hamish as a possibility is that one of his wives once called him James and Hamish is the Gaelic form of James, so it may have been an ethnic slip on her part. Also, he had a brother named Henry, who was an alcoholic. Watson was born in 1852 in Hampshire. His mother died in his infancy, and he moved with his father to Australia. He returned to England, studied medicine at Bart's (St. Bartholomew Hospital), then at the army surgical school at Netley, and was attached to the Fifth Northumberland Fusiliers as assistant surgeon. The regiment was already deep in enemy country in India, but shortly after joining it, Watson was removed from his brigade and attached to the Berkshires, with whom he served at the battle of Maiwand. In this battle, Watson was wounded by a Jezail bullet from the "murderous Ghazis." That brings us to another really contested point. Where was he wounded? The wound is mentioned, I think, five times, several times as in the hip (a nice euphemism) and also as in the shoulder. A Bostonian scholar figured out how it happened. Watson must have been drunk. His faithful orderly, Murray, saw his condition and threw him over a beast of burden, which would explain how the bullet went in one end and out the other.

Watson was married two times, maybe three. I am of the two-times school. He married Mary Morstan from *The Sign of the Four*, and she conveniently died so that he could go back to Holmes. Then he married again, perhaps Violet de Merville.

Stephen Benét called Watson "my favorite character." A. A. Milne wrote two eloquent essays defending him. And let me say parenthetically that although Watson has often been unfairly ridiculed, the character assassination of the Watson characterization in the Universal Pictures, with Rathbone and Bruce, is simply a disgrace. Watson was not a bumbling fool.[2] Here's what Holmes had to say about Watson—and Holmes was never flattering:

> "Really, Watson, you excel yourself,...I am bound to say that in all the accounts which you have been so good as to give of my own small achievements you have habitually underrated your own abilities. It may be that you are not yourself luminous, but you are a conductor of light."

2. Indeed not! He was an important part of the agency; see, "Are There Others."—Ed.

Watson's fame rests upon his conducting the light of Sherlock Holmes. He wrote fifty-six of the sixty stories that we have. Two that were written by Holmes himself are very poor. Mycroft wrote one, "His Last Bow," and Arthur Conan Doyle wrote one, "The Mazarin Stone."

Now Arthur Conan Doyle you may have heard of also. He was a writer of historical novels, rather good ones, and of various other works of fiction; and he wrote, I think, nineteen books and pamphlets on spiritualism. He was born in 1859, and he died in 1930. Doyle was a medical doctor, though not a successful one, and he was Watson's agent. He's famous for two other things. He introduced skiing into Switzerland and thus is considered the father of skiing as a sport, and he spent a quarter of a million pounds to prove spirit photography.

The first story in the Canon, as we call the writings, is *A Study in Scarlet,* which appeared in *Beeton's Christmas Annual,* 1887. It had been sold outright for twenty-five pounds, which was then $125; there has been no other income from it to the Doyle estate. The story didn't sell, and was in danger of ending the series almost before it began. But luckily the whole thing was saved by an agent for *Lippincott's Magazine* from Philadelphia. Someone there who liked it commissioned more stories, and the world is the richer for it. So is the estate.

The four long stories are: *The Hound of the Baskervilles,* the best of all, I think; *The Valley of Fear,* much of which is laid in Pennsylvania; *The Sign of the Four;* and *A Study in Scarlet,* which is partly about the Mormons in Utah. These stories have sold about ten million copies in hard cover, and an incredible number of copies in various bindings — many millions. They have been translated into forty-seven languages that we know about. Recently it was discovered that they have been translated into Frisian, and now, of course, the chase is on to get the Frisian edition. The Doyle estate is the largest literary estate in history.

There have been more than 150 Sherlock Holmes movies, more than seventy-five TV productions, and more than twenty plays. A fine play now going the rounds in both colleges and little theaters was written by John Fenn of Minneapolis. It is called *Sherlock Holmes and the Affair of the Amorous Regent.*

There have been more books, pamphlets, monographs, studies,

essays, addresses, parodies, and pastiches published about Holmes than about anyone else. There are Sherlock Holmes games, puzzles, songs, toys, cigars, postage stamps, pubs, and tours: and of course there are countless jokes about the great detective. There have been two musicals and one ballet (with very pleasant music by a contemporary British composer). And of all things, there is a stained glass Sherlock Holmes window in the College of St. Thomas library in St. Paul. There are Sherlock Holmes designs in needlepoint. I may mention that my wife did in crewel embroidery the curtains in my library, which represent my four favorite stories. There are various ephemeral things such as jewelry. I have, for instance, cufflinks made from the brass buttons on the uniforms of Watson's regiment. The tie I am wearing bears the insignia of the London society.

Then there are the writings about the writings. At least seven periodicals are devoted entirely to this subject. *The Baker Street Journal,* the publication of The Baker Street Irregulars, has a circulation list of over 2,000. It is published by Fordham University Press, and is in its twenty-eighth year. *The Sherlock Holmes Journal* of London, which is an answer to the American one, is more staid and scholarly; it is in its twenty-third year. A periodical called *Sherlockiana,* published in Denmark, will be in its twenty-fifth year in January. There is an annual published in Stockholm called *The Baker Street Cab Lantern.* Chicago has the *Devon County Chronicle* and a new magazine called *Baker Street Miscellanea,* which promises to be an exceedingly good publication. San Francisco has the *Vermissa Herald.* A number of such publications are in limbo. In Sherlockian groups, the publications depend mainly on the condition of the thyroid of the person in charge.

The critical material about Holmes really began to be composed as early as 1905.[3] (One earlier thing I have is a song written at Edinburgh University and published in the student annual in 1892: a burlesque of Holmes.) In 1905, a British publisher, Sedgwick Jackson, pointed out the obvious fact that Watson was hell on dates; he just was chronologically inept. But the great piece of incunabula in any Holmes library was published in 1912. Ronald Knox (later Monsignor Ronald Knox and author of what I still think the best

---

3. The earliest "incunabulum" included in Edgar W. Smith, ed., *The Incunabular Sherlock Holmes,* (Morristown, N.J., 1958) was by Arthur Maurice, dated 1902. –Ed.

literary translation of the Bible) gave a speech at the Oxford Union called "Studies in the Literature of Sherlock Holmes." It was actually composed as a satire on theologians; he poked fun at their nit-picking, and to do so he nitpicked Holmes. He was asked to give that talk again and again. It was published in 1912 in the *Oxford Blue Book,* and I'm happy to inform the librarians present that I have a copy. And I'm going to keep it.

There are six or seven biographies of Sherlock Holmes, more than of many people one might expect to be better known. Vincent Starrett, book editor of the *Chicago Tribune,* did the best of the biographies, *The Private Life of Sherlock Holmes,* in 1933. It's out now in an excellent paperback edition with annotations about Starrett, who was a great literary man. S. C. Roberts, who was a master of Pembroke College, also wrote a biography. William Baring-Gould, an editor of *Time,* wrote *Sherlock Holmes of Baker Street.* I must warn you that it's a bit fanciful. Most Holmesians stick strictly to fact, as I do myself, but Baring-Gould sometimes was carried away. He even published a photograph of Holmes, and there is no known photograph of him. There is also a biography in Japanese, and one in German. There is a biography of Watson and even a biography of Moriarty; it's significant that there is none of Irene Adler. There are a number of chronologies of the stories: sources of considerable debate, since Watson displays great inconsistencies in the dating of the cases. An incredible bibliography has recently come out, the work of a Colorado librarian, Ronald De Waal: *The World Bibliography of Sherlock Holmes and Dr. Watson.* It lists 12,000 items. He has worked in my house eight days so far on his first supplement, and it will contain another 3,000 items.

There have been pamphlets and articles on Holmes and dogs, Holmes and horses, Holmes and the weather, Holmes's health. One notorious paper about Holmes has never been published; some of us are trying to find the widow of the man who wrote it so as to get permission to publish it. The author, who was both a doctor and a lawyer, worked many years analyzing Holmes's disposition, finally determining that it was influenced by bad health, the result of faulty elimination, because Holmes ate very badly (sporadically and with no roughage). Several dermatologists have written on Holmes, and there is now a professional organization for Sherlockians within the dermatological profession, called The Sir James Saunders Society. Dr. Goodman, the only living member from the first Baker Street

John Bennett
Shaw, B.S.I.

Irregular dinner, spent many years writing an article proving that Holmes's personality was affected by bad teeth. There are several studies of Holmes and tobacco, Holmes and drugs. As you know, Holmes at one time took cocaine in a seven percent solution; there's no denying it. One man at Yale, after long study, came up with the conclusion that a seven percent solution was not addictive.

There are articles on food and drink in the Holmes stories. I did an article in which I analyzed 176 meals mentioned in the Canon. I concluded that Holmes was a gourmet, but a very sporadic one, subject to many other influences. A real gourmet never lets business or anything else interfere with his pleasure, but Holmes did. Watson didn't. Watson didn't give a damn what he ate as long as he ate it, which I think was probably the British view. There are Holmes atlases, accounts of Holmes and the railroad, etc. Three coats of arms for Holmes have been published. You can find an argument that Holmes was Jewish, as well as an argument that he was anti-Semitic. There are studies of his religion; his prayer has been published, a dull non-sectarian sort of thing. A very fine full-length book deals with Holmes and music. One woman holds the theory that he was one of the inventors of the twelve-tone scale—along with Hindemith and several others.

The parodies and pastiches are interesting. Approximately 130 cases are mentioned in the Canon that were not written up, and every one of them has been written by somebody else, some as many as ten or twelve times. The best imitations, I think, are the Solar Pons stories, by August Derleth. I have in my collection more than 600 parodies. Then there is the science-fictional Sherlock Holmes. There's one piece I always like to mention (it's in an anthology called *The Science Fictional Sherlock Holmes*). The story is about the world being devastated with an atomic bomb, with just a few pockets of civilization left. One of the survivors is an Arizona aircraft engineer. After 200 years his descendants build a plane and start flying east from Arizona. They find another group of people in Arkansas, but these are like Stone Age men by this time, and they drive the newcomers off. The same thing happens in Ohio, but there's a group around Pittsburgh (where much of the university is underground) that has preserved one book which is now their Bible: the Sherlock Holmes Canon. Sam Rosenberg, who wrote *Naked Is the Best Disguise* (a fascinating book if you don't take it seriously) maintained, after going as my guest to the Baker Street Irregular dinner in New York and visiting with the Sherlockians, that we probably are the germ of the next great religion.

John Bennett
Shaw, B.S.I.

There are many poems in praise of Holmes. T. S. Eliot wrote a marvelous poem about Moriarty called "Macavity the Mystery Cat." There are countless borrowings and allusions in modern writers; you have to know Holmes to know modern literature. There are annual horse races associated with the great racing story "Silver Blaze": at Arlington (Chicago), Belmont (New York), in Washington and in Canada and in Denmark.

Now for the societies. Nowhere else is there such a disorganized organization of people espousing such a cause: "keeping green the memory of the master detective," as Christopher Morley put it. The parent society is The Baker Street Irregulars, organized in New York in 1934. Frank Morley, the brother of Christopher Morley (then an editor of *The Saturday Review of Literature*) was on his way back to England, and to entertain himself he made up a Sherlock Holmes crossword puzzle. (No mean task; my wife did one a few years ago with 210 Sherlockian definitions.) Chris published his brother's puzzle. He liked societies, and he loved Holmes, so he said that those who had more-or-less correct answers would be invited to the first dinner of a new society called The Baker Street Irregulars. Well, there were twenty-three, I think, that qualified. And a number came. One was a woman, but she soon married and moved to Ohio. That took care of that. But women weren't really eliminated. Chris Morley's daughter, who lives in Santa Fe, has told me that she went to one of the dinners, but this, you know, is one of those things that happen that you don't talk about.

There are probably more than 100 societies such as The Norwegian Explorers in the United States. They are loosely organized, or not organized at all. Technically, a society is supposed to clear its name with The Baker Street Irregulars; it can then call itself a scion society. The London society started right at the same time as The Baker Street Irregulars, and it certainly is not a scion. These two societies are separate but equal. World War II interfered with the British group, but they reorganized in 1951 and they're going strong now.

The Baker Street Irregulars met for a long time at a restaurant called Christ Cella's—not because the food was good, but because the restaurant had seventeen steps, the number of steps to Holmes's rooms in Baker Street. They've moved around, but met every year

John Bennett
Shaw, B.S.I.

on January 6, or the nearest Friday to that date, to celebrate Holmes's birthday. They always have formal toasts. Women are not admitted; but around 1961, some of the consciences began to hurt a little, and since Holmes admired Irene Adler and was defeated by her, and since the first stated toast is to her as *"the* woman," a woman was invited to receive that first toast. She's given two drinks (if she drinks quickly) and a corsage, and then is spirited away. Last year the only remaining daughter of Conan Doyle, Princess Mdivani, was the fourteenth woman to receive the toast. My wife was the thirteenth. The reason Dorothy did it is that the women get a pin showing the doorway of 221B Baker Street. No man has a copy of that, and I have to outlive her to get it.

I think that the Constitution and Buy-laws of The Baker Street Irregulars are a model. If we adopted these articles nationally, we wouldn't even have to have Sam Ervin to interpret them:

CONSTITUTION

ARTICLE I
The name of this society shall be The Baker Street Irregulars.

ARTICLE II
Its purpose shall be the study of the Sacred Writings.

ARTICLE III
All persons shall be eligible for membership who pass an examination in the Sacred Writings set by officers of the society, and who are considered otherwise suitable.

ARTICLE IV
The officers shall be a Gosogene, a Tantalus, and a Commissionaire.

The duties of the Gasogene shall be those commonly performed by a President.

The duties of the Tantalus shall be those commonly performed by a Secretary.

The duties of a Commissionaire shall be to telephone down for ice, White Rock, and whatever else may be required and available; to conduct all negotiations with waiters; and to assess the members pro rata for the cost of same.

BUY-LAWS
1. An annual meeting shall be held on January 6, at which the canonical toasts shall be drunk;[4] after which the members shall drink at will.

4. The canonical toasts are to *"the* woman," "Mrs. Hudson," "Mycroft," and Dr. Watson's second wife.

2. The current round shall be bought by any member who fails to identify, by title of story and context, any quotation from the Sacred Writings submitted by any other member.

John Bennett
Shaw, B.S.I.

> *Qualification A.* If two or more members fail so to identify, a round shall be bought by each of those so failing.

> *Qualification B.* If the submitter of the quotation, upon challenge, fails to identify it correctly, he shall buy the round.

3. Special meetings may be called at any time or place by any one of three members, two of whom shall constitute a quorum.

> *Qualification A.* If said two people are of opposite sexes, they shall use care in selecting the place of meeting, to avoid misinterpretation (or interpretation either, for that matter).

4. All other business shall be left for the monthly meeting.

5. There shall be no monthly meeting.

This parent organization, with 170 or so members, has operated ever since 1934 without a rift. Of the many scion societies in this country, The Speckled Band of Boston is probably the oldest, though their claim is disputed. They give an annual prize for drama, and have had some remarkable things in that line, including a delightful musical about Wilson, the canary trainer — with a chorus of canaries.

In Chicago are The Hounds of the Baskerville *(sic)*. The reason for their complicated name is that early on a pirated edition of *The Hound* was published in Chicago with a misspelled title. They have a number of functions, now shared with Hugo's Companions, including the horse race at Arlington. Hugo's Companions is named after the drunken companions of Hugo Baskerville. The head of this organization, which has about sixty members, is called the Most Drunken Companion. Since I now live in New Mexico, I am the Most Distant Companion. They meet nine times a year. A group in Washington, The Red Circle, started out seemingly anti-feminine, even though it was a woman who originally thought of organizing it. So a woman in the State Department formed her own group, called The Solitary Cyclist; she met by herself every year at the Willard Hotel bar. The Red Circle is now a large group including many women. Among their founding members was Lord Paul Gore-Booth, until recently the permanent foreign secretary, and formerly President of the London Society. This group once invited J. Edgar Hoover to a meeting. Of course, it utterly confused him. And they got an incredible letter from him saying, in effect, "Gosh, you guys are sure nice to invite me. What do you do?"

John Bennett
Shaw, B.S.I.

The Copper Beeches of Philadelphia is another long established and distinguished group. There's a good mystery novel about them, *Copper Beeches,* by Arthur H. Lewis. Unfortunately, they have a waiting list of about twice the number they have in membership.

A striking thing about Sherlockians: if you don't get into a group or don't like a group you start your own. We're really irregular. A group in Cleveland called The Creeping Men put out a little newspaper called *All The News That's Fit to Creep.* There's a group in Kansas City called The Great Alkali Plainsmen, which began as a typical Holmesian group. The founders published a quiz in the paper, and those who answered it got in. Of course, it was going to be strictly a men's organization. The winner of the quiz was M. W. Weis, and M. W. Weis turned out to be a very tall, willowy high-school girl. She was one of the best members in those days. This society also has a curious anomaly in the Holmesian world: a tee-totaler member. They could take him around and exhibit him. The worst thing about him is that he's proud of it. He's a librarian, too, which makes it doubly bad.

A group in Nebraska is called The Maiwand Jezails, after the battle in which Watson was wounded. One of our projects, yes I am a member, is to buy a statue to erect on the site (not the spot where Watson was shot, which would be too anatomical, but on the site of the battle). We have had great difficulty with the Afghani government, because it said we could do nothing in any way favorable to the British. Then we agreed that we would merely have a Jezail soldier pointing his gun sort of down, so that it would hit Watson where it was supposed to have hit him; and that was agreeable. But they had a turnover in the government a couple of years ago, and our money is still in a Swiss bank. We don't know what to do. Next summer, two of our professors (you know, professors are a strange breed) are going to Afghanistan with an inflatable monument, and they're going to blow it up and run.

In Detroit there are two societies, as well as a ladies' group that was started in protest called The Friends of Lizzie Borden (they go out every year and chop a tree down).

One Detroit scion, The Amateur Mendicants, is named after a group mentioned in one of the stories which met in the basement of a deserted warehouse. So this group has their annual dinner in the basement of a deserted warehouse. It's a formal dinner, catered; and to get to it they have to go down an alley in their dinner jackets, surrounded by winos, and down a creaky, dirty stairway. It is reported that, once, the police couldn't stand it and raided them. This society held another memorable meeting at the faculty club of Detroit University. Sixteen members were present, and each one brought a dog that he thought was the prototype of the Hound of the Baskervilles. Each had only three minutes to prove his point. Unhappily, the member who brought a dachshund won. The dogs wrecked the faculty club. One dog bit the maitre d'; another did something naughty. And the next day there was a nicely lettered sign that is now in the archives of the society: "The Amateur Mendicant Society will no longer be welcome at the Faculty Club."

In Tulsa, my old home, a new society was started. I hope I planted the seed before I left, several years ago. It is called The Afghanistan Perceivers, because when Holmes first met Watson, he said, "You have been in Afghanistan, I perceive." The Perceivers have a nice insignia: just a big eye looking at you. They did a great thing last August. They had discovered a little town named Watson, Oklahoma, (population 137) down in the Ozarks, almost to the Arkansas border. They got a group from Tulsa and Oklahoma City and Little Rock, went over there by bus, and had a ceremony commemorating the ninety-third anniversary of the Battle of Maiwand. They ran up the British flag, and had several pipers dressed in British uniforms come down the street. Not one local person came out of his house.

I should mention the women's lib group which started out to counter The Baker Street Irregulars. A group of thirteen women at Albertus Magnus College in New Haven, crosstown from Yale, wanted to start a Sherlockian society. They wrote to me. I have been and am an advisor to a national college group—fifty or a hundred guys and gals all over the country. I suggested that since Holmes had a fondness for the name Violet (I believe eight or nine characters in the Canon are named Violet),[5] they call themselves The Shrinking Violets. But they named themselves instead the Adventuresses of Sherlock Holmes.

This group picketed the Baker Street dinner, at Cavanagh's on 23rd Street. The temperature was 17°. Six of these women showed up with huge banners reading "BSI unfair to women everywhere." The Commissionaire of The Baker Street Irregulars said, "Shaw,

5. We hope Mr. Shaw will write up the "Adventure of the Missing Violets," for while he notes that there were 8 or 9 Violets, we have been able to locate only four.–Ed."

your crazy girls are downstairs. What are we going to do? The press is there!" And the press *was* there. WRTV had the story and so did a *New York Times* reporter, but I'm happy to report that one can still influence the *Times*, because it never appeared in print.

The women never let it be known that they had consulted with me, and that I had said, "Go to it." But I did read their statement for the group, and of course it produced the biggest booing I've ever received. The next year they tried to crash the cocktail party. Now they're going to start having a dinner counter to the Baker Street dinner.

Seriously, women should be members, of course, provided that they are qualified Sherlockians, not because they are spouses of members. And several of us who hope to have a bigger voice when some of the old ones go to their reward in the Baker Street up there also hope that we can see that ten or twelve or fifteen or more women we know who are really qualified Sherlockians will become members.

There's a society in Little Rock, Arkansas, called The Arkansas Valley Investors, after the place where the imaginary Alexander Hamilton Garrideb was supposed to have made all his money. A couple of student groups have nice names. One is called The Baker Street Irrationals. There are also The Baker Street Underground, The Pageboys, The Board School Beacons, The Bullpups, and The Goose Club. A serious group of Sherlockians in Portland, called The Noble and Most Singular Order of the Blue Carbuncle, issues a newsletter called *Feathers from the Nest*.

One of the more interesting groups is one that Dorothy and I started in Santa Fe. It is called The Brothers Three of Moriarty. There is a town named Moriarty in New Mexico. So we felt it was a natural, and we formed a group which meets once a year on Moriarty's birthday or approximately, which appropriately is the time we usually get our first winter storm, and the roads are very dangerous. We meet in the back room of a little old bar. The street is often a mudhole. There's no food except frozen sandwiches called astronauts, most logically. (Moriarty wrote a book called *The Dynamics of an Asteroid,* which Einstein used in his calculations.) Our insignia consists of three *J*'s, after the three brothers, all named James. The middle *J* is crooked.

I'm not going to talk about The Norwegian Explorers—you know about them.[6] In Denmark is a remarkable organization called

---

6. We regret this decision of Mr. Shaw's, appropriate as it was at the time, since he was speaking to a gathering of Explorers, but depriving us of the additional advertising we would have welcomed. Those desirous of same are encouraged to consult Dr. Crawford's "Introduction."–Ed.

the Sherlock Holmes Klubben i Danmark. They have met several times a year for twenty-five years. The Baritsu Society of Hong Kong has a branch in Tokyo. Dr. Naganuma of Tokyo, head of the branch, has done seven books on Holmes which unfortunately are in Japanese. There's a society in Holland and another in Sweden. Another group devoted to the memory of one of the evil men in the Canon is called The Milvertonians of Hampstead, named after Charles Augustus Milverton, the evil blackmailer, who lived there. To be a member you have to live within a fifteen-minute walk of Hampstead.

25

John Bennett
Shaw, B.S.I.

I should mention the collections. You have here in your University Library the McDiarmid collection of Holmes material, which is quite good. There's a remarkable collection at the Metropolitan Central Library in Toronto. Originally, most of it belonged to Judge S. Tupper Bigelow, a Baker Street Irregular. I have what is probably the largest of all research collections, with ten or twelve thousand Holmes items. I have a room that was built just to house my collection, and I must report that it's almost full and I don't know what I'm going to do.

There are a great many Holmes jokes. Dr. Clendenning, a Kansas City Sherlockian, wrote the remarkable little story about Holmes dying and going to heaven and God saying, "I'm so glad you're here. I desperately need you. We're having a big celebration, and we can't find Adam." And Holmes went out and came back in two hours with a man, and said, "This is Adam." And God said, "How did you know?" Holmes said, "Elementary. No navel." And then there's the famous story: Holmes said, "Ah, Watson, I see that you've put on your winter underwear." Watson said, "Good God, man, how did you know that?" And Holmes said, "You forgot your trousers." Probably the most famous witticism about Holmes was composed by Doyle's brother-in-law, E. W. Hornung, who wrote the delightful Raffles stories. He said, "Be they ever so humble, there's no police like Holmes."

A nice point: the 14th edition of the *Britannica* had a listing of all the persons mentioned in it, and the real people were in boldface and the fictional characters in italics. Holmes was in boldface.

People always ask me, "Why do you do this?" I could say that the reason I give a talk like this is that it's the only chance I get to talk without being argued with—but really, why *do* all of us do this? During World War II, Vincent Starrett wrote a sonnet that I think sums up the whole thing. It's called "221B."

John Bennett
Shaw, B.S.I.

Here dwell together still two men of note
Who never lived and so can never die:
How very near they seem, yet how remote
That age before the world went all awry.
But still the game's afoot for those with ears
Attuned to catch the distant view-halloo:
England is England yet, for all our fears—
Only those things the heart believes are true.

A yellow fog swirls past the window-pane
As night descends upon this fabled street;
A lonely hansom splashes through the rain,
The ghostly gas lamps fail at twenty feet.
Here, though the world explode, these two survive,
And it is always eighteen ninety-five.

ARE THERE OTHERS?
Sherlock Holmes's Opinion of Watson
E. W. McDiarmid B.S.I.

"WATSON, I have always done you an injustice. There are others."
This remark by Sherlock Holmes in "The Adventure of the Three
Students" must be one of the most cutting remarks in all of the
Canon. What is the occasion? Holmes is a bit miffed because Mr.
Hilton Soames cannot follow the implications of the pencil chip with
the letters NN remaining. What Holmes is in effect saying may be
something like this: "I have always thought you, Watson, to be the
slowest(?), densest(?), dumbest(?) person, but now I can see that
there are others equally so." Does this really represent the Master's
opinion of his "friend and colleague"?

Other than references throughout Watson's reporting, perhaps
the most extensive comment on Watson by Holmes himself is contained in "The Blanched Soldier" which Holmes is reported to have
written:

> Speaking of my old friend and biographer, I would
> take this opportunity to remark that if I burden myself
> with a companion in my various little inquiries it is not
> done out of sentiment or caprice, but it is that Watson
> has some remarkable characteristics of his own to
> which in his modesty he has given small attention amid
> his exaggerated estimates of my own performances. A
> confederate who foresees your conclusions and course
> of action is always dangerous, but one to whom each
> development comes as a perpetual surprise, and to
> whom the future is always a closed book, is, indeed, an
> ideal helpmate.

Not fulsome praise to be sure, yet certainly more restrained than the
"there are others" comment—yet even so the implication of
Holmes's statement is certainly not overly complimentary to Watson's perspicacity.

Are these two comments typical? Do they reflect Holmes's opin-
ion of Watson accurately? The only sure answer is to be found in the
Sacred Writings. What follows is an attempt to record and classify
Sherlockian comments which illustrate Holmes's opinion of Watson.

There are a total of fifty-nine comments by Holmes which in my
judgment reflect his opinion of Watson. Perhaps others would clas-

E. W.
McDiarmid
B.S.I.

sify them differently, include some that I omit, or weed out some that I include, but to me they can be grouped into three categories:

    A. Facetious and not serious

    B. Obviously uncomplimentary

    C. Obviously complimentary

I omit such phrases as "my old friend Watson," "my dear fellow," and "the good Doctor." Though they reflect a warm relationship, they do not indicate Holmes's opinion of Watson's ability.

    I am sure true Sherlockians would relish the chance of reviewing fifty-nine quotations with an extended description of the circumstances surrounding each. However, to do so would result in an overly long account. Thus one must be selective, i.e., indicate only briefly the context where relevant.

    Holmes is not often facetious in his remarks. Actually of the ten remarks so recorded, six occur in two adventures, "The Missing Three-Quarter," and *The Valley of Fear*. Here are typical examples, first from *The Valley of Fear*:

> "You are developing a certain unexpected vein of pawky humor"
>
> "Your native shrewdness, my dear Watson..."
>
> "One more coruscation..."

From "The Missing Three-Quarter":

> "Your reflection, though profound, had already crossed my mind"
>
> "Excellent, Watson! You are scintillating..."
>
> "With all respect for your natural acumen."

Actually less reflections of Holmes's opinion of Watson than attempts to be facetious, these throw little light on the Master's judgment of his friend. Watson could well have replied, "You are developing a certain vein of pawky humour." Perhaps one could argue here that the implications are uncomplimentary, but the fact that in each of these instances Watson felt no irritation suggests that they were merely badinage.

    On the contrary, in the nine uncomplimentary remarks I have been able to identify, Watson, where he has the opportunity, reveals irritation or disagreement. Thus when Holmes says, "You have done remarkably badly," Watson replies with some heat, "What should I have done?" In "The Retired Colourman" Holmes remarks, "It is true that though in your mission you have missed everything of importance..." Watson then retaliates with these words: "what have I missed?" to which Holmes responds as was his wont, to the feeling rather than the words, "Don't be hurt, my dear fellow."

Obviously, Watson has no opportunity to reply to Holmes's account from "The Blanched Soldier" quoted earlier, and in "The Three Students," the "there are others" comment is followed by a long explanation of the significance of the letters NN remaining on the pencil chip, giving Watson no chance to react.

But there is another characteristic of the uncomplimentary comments. Almost without exception they are occasioned by Watson's preference for action rather than reflection, as for instance in "The Disappearance of Lady Frances Carfax," "a very pretty hash you have made of it." Holmes recognizes this when he says in *The Hound of the Baskervilles,* "you were born to be a man of action."

Many of the forty complimentary remarks commend Watson for being a man of action: "there is no prospect of danger, or I should not dream of stirring out without you," and "I knew you would not shrink at the last." Though not always accompanied by comments from Holmes, the obvious pleasure which he feels at being accompanied by Watson is clearly recorded in the Canon. Holmes respects Watson as a man of action.

Holmes makes a point of the importance of observation and deduction and there are numerous compliments on Watson's ability, "You can thank Dr. Watson's observation for that," and "another of Dr. Watson's bull's-eyes," and "capital, Watson! a thumb nail sketch." And although the implication of some of the uncomplimentary remarks is that Watson does not make obvious deductions, there is evidence to the contrary: "Well, Watson, I will not offend your intelligence by explaining what is obvious," "if my friend would undertake it," and "the faculty of deduction is certainly contagious."

To recount all of the complimentary remarks regarding Watson's personal qualities would extend this discussion too long, for example:

"The very soul of discretion"

"A trusty comrade"

"There is a delightful freshness about you"

"You won't fail me, you never did fail me."

But perhaps this was summed up best by Holmes's comment in "The Abbey Grange":

"Watson, you are a British jury, and I never met a man who was more eminently fitted to represent one."

To me the most telling of Holmes's remarks about Watson are the numerous occasions when he makes it clear that Watson is a part of the team. This is alluded to in Holmes's explanation of why he "burdens" himself with a companion, but is more specifically evident in no fewer than thirteen references such as:

"our data"

"some cards in our hands"

"This is my intimate friend and associate"

"open all notes and telegrams, and to act on your own judgment."

Thus we see Watson as an intimate "friend and partner," one whose observation is valuable, whose discretion is perfect, whose love of action is evident, and who represents in the finest way the fairness of a British jury.

While Holmes seems to delight in lecturing Watson on his limitations as a writer, he recognizes his own limitations: "I am lost without my Boswell." And in this connection as in the case of the ten facetious remarks and the nine uncomplimentary ones there are extenuating circumstances: a jocular mood, frustration at a case going badly, or irritation at being separated from the congenial surroundings of Baker Street.

It is in the overwhelming majority of complimentary remarks that we see the true evaluation which Holmes places on his friend and companion. No better testimony could be offered than Holmes's outburst when Killer Evans's bullet grazes Watson's thigh, "You're not hurt, Watson? For God's sake, say that you are not hurt!"

HOLMES: THE POTENTIAL ENTREPRENEUR
Ronald M. Hubbs

THE INVIGORATING CHALLENGE in a business career is problem solving. Success depends upon it. Readers of the Canon know that one of the greatest problem solvers who ever lived was Sherlock Holmes. And what a batting average he had!

Holmes remarked in "The Five Orange Pips": "I have been beaten four times—three times by men and once by a woman." If our research begins and ends with the disclosed cases in the Canon, there are only four failures out of sixty cases reported.[1] Counting "The Veiled Lodger" as a "no contest," out of 59 scorable cases we produce a success rate of 93.2%. Fabulous!

The dictionary says an entrepreneur is "a person who organizes and manages any enterprise, especially a business, usually with considerable initiative and risk." Application of this definition to Holmes is immediate and obvious. The "business" part equates with his unexploited talent as an entrepreneur.

Condensed from *News Front* is this representative list of personality traits for the successful businessman: drive for achievement; dissatisfaction with mediocrity; decisiveness; confidence; sense of personal responsibility; self-discipline; organizational ability (bringing order out of chaos by relating seemingly isolated facts or events); and ability to handle people (inspire their respect and enlist their cooperation as did Holmes with Scotland Yard, Baker Street Irregulars, clients, and chance acquaintances).

In the magazine *Money,* two psychologists propose questions to reveal entrepreneurial attitudes. One of the questions is: "In your daydreams would you most likely appear as (a) a millionaire floating on a yacht, (b) a detective who has solved a difficult case, (c) a politician giving an election night victory speech?" Naturally, the right answer is b. We are making progress.

But if you argue that Holmes had no training for business specifically, then you should heed Socrates who said to Nicomachides: "Over whatever a man may preside, he will, if he knows what he needs and is able to provide, be a good president, whether he have the direction of a chorus, a family, a city, or an army."

1. Frank J. Eustace, Jr., "Sherlock Meets the Analyst" in *Leaves From the Copper Beeches,* Narberth, Pa., 1959.

It is well known that an entrepreneur, a business executive, a good manager—has abilities that can be transferred readily from one sphere to another. Holmes with all of his cited attributes and brilliance would be marked for success almost irrespective of his direction.

What attributes for business success did Holmes display? For example, he was a decision maker, an achiever who strove for excellence. He was imaginative, tireless; persevering; analytical. He gave attention to detail and could conceptualize and was willing to assume risk (courage). One can be encyclopedic about this. Let us look at some examples from the Canon.

Characteristics of the problem solver, the relentless driver, can be seen in Watson's words in *The Sign of the Four:* "You really are an automaton—a calculating machine....There is something positively inhuman in you at times." And Stamford in *A Study in Scarlet* pays tribute to Holmes's learning with: "...he has amassed a lot of out-of-the-way knowledge which would astonish his professors."

From "A Scandal in Bohemia" we learn that "He was, I take it, the most perfect reasoning and observing machine that the world has seen...." And what marketing organization wouldn't drool to have Holmes after this: "It was difficult to refuse any of Sherlock Holmes's requests, for they were always so exceedingly definite, and put forward with such a quiet air of mastery." ("The Man with the Twisted Lip")

Sherlock Holmes's ability to solve problems was repeatedly noticed. In "The Speckled Band" our friend Dr. Watson observes: "I had no keener pleasure than in following Holmes in his professional investigations, and in admiring the rapid deductions, as swift as intuitions, and yet always founded on a logical basis, with which he unravelled the problems which were submitted to him." Then in "The Five Orange Pips" we see this: Openshaw: "He said that you could solve anything." Holmes: "He said too much."

None of this is to suggest Holmes would not have problems as an entrepreneur. Indeed he would. It is the lot of all business executives. In the case of the Master at least two might be suspected: planning and coping, with women.

Good executives and entrepreneurs are good planners. In many ways Holmes was a superb planner. But with large organizations and in many situations the technique requires close cooperation with others. Watson was moved to record in *The Hound of the Baskervilles:* "One of Sherlock Holmes's defects...was that he was exceedingly loth to communicate his full plans to any other person until the instant of their fulfillment."

Because women are increasingly more important in the business world, it is easy to assume that the Master would have rough going in the commercial community if his attitude towards women was as sometimes erroneously represented. But we needn't fret about this because Holmes was not a misogynist.

A notorious attribution to Holmes that "women are never to be entirely trusted" is often so warped out of context that it gives Holmes an undeserved blemish. Actually the remark arose from good natured banter between Holmes and Watson in *The Sign of the Four* as Watson announces he is going calling. The dialogue is this:

> "On Mrs. Cecil Forrester?" asked Holmes with the twinkle of a smile in his eyes.
> "Well, of course on Miss Morstan, too. They were anxious to hear what happened."
> "I would not tell them too much," said Holmes. "Women are never to be entirely trusted—not the best of them."
> I did not pause to argue over this atrocious sentiment.

Both Holmes and Watson understood this friendly and sly dig. Watson's obvious infatuation with Miss Morstan resulted in her becoming the second Mrs. Watson.[2] So it was a mischievous remark intended not to be taken seriously. Holmes should not be lashed for that statement.

Although some male chauvinists may be surprised, women were employed extensively in many industries and businesses that were flourishing during Holmes's most productive years. The noted British economic historian Henry Hamilton says "...during the three decades before the First World War...the sphere of women's employment enormously widened."[3] Hence, it would be important for Holmes in a successful business career to be in rapport with the opposite sex.

S. C. Roberts in "Sherlock Holmes and the Fair Sex" (H. W. Bell, ed., *Baker Street Studies*, 1955) has countless examples of sympathy,

2. Mr. Hubbs obviously accepts Mr. Baring-Gould's statement that Mary Morstan was Watson's second wife. As Mr. Shaw notes, there is dispute over this matter.—Ed.

3. W. H. Hamilton, *England—History of the Homeland*, New York, 1948, p. 338.

compassion, and helpfulness — yes, tenderness — accorded women by Holmes. There is a considerable body of evidence that he was interested in women and indeed affectionate, thoughtful, and sensitive for the distressed. He also rated highly the intuitive judgment of women in "The Man with the Twisted Lip" with these words: "I have seen too much not to know that the impression of a woman may be more valuable than the conclusion of an analytical reasoner." Women? No — there was no trouble here for Holmes in the business world.

If Holmes were so well qualified for a business life, the crucial question is: Why wasn't this Holmes's choice? Let us examine four possible reasons: 1) ancestral background, 2) money, 3) early commitment as a consulting detective, 4) love of his work.

Michael Harrison in the article "The Blue Blood of the Holmeses," *Baker Street Journal*, v.14, no.2 (June, 1964) tells us the Master was of an ennobled family, even though the peerage had not descended to him. Was it this uncomfortable knowledge that caused him to insist in "The Greek Interpreter" that "My ancestors were country squires, who appear to have led much the same life as is natural to their class."

At the time of Holmes the nobility was finding its way into the marts of trade and the merchants were inching into the realms of the privileged classes. Fortunes were being made then in England and both classes were impacting on each other. Hamilton puts it: "The wealthy merchant did not storm the citadel of privilege. He sought entry by purchase of an estate, by marriage, or by winning a peerage."[4]

But with it all the landed gentry still was the most prestigious in England. Going into trade was by no means the most desirable vocation. If Holmes had been born at a later time, his ancestral background might not have been a handicap to entering business, at least in his own mind. His possible claim to a peerage, or as a descendant of land owners, may have restrained him from seeking success as a business entrepreneur.

The influence of money in the life of Sherlock Holmes is a fascinating topic. A disinterest in financial incentives per se would not have been a barrier to a business career. Many studies disprove money as a prime mover in the ambitions of most entrepreneurs, but to the extent it is of influence, what about it in the case of Holmes?

4. Hamilton, *ibid.*, p.262.

Holmes's alleged aloofness to money is found in his "My professional charges are upon a fixed scale....I do not vary them, save
when I remit them altogether." ("Thor Bridge") R. K. Leavitt in
"Nummi in Arca or the Fiscal Holmes" (Vincent Starrett, *221-B
Studies in Sherlock Holmes,* New York, 1956) says this statement
is a "bare-faced falsehood" to "put the blustery, purse-proud Yankee
(the Gold King, Senator Neil Gibson) in his place...."

Leavitt also reports Holmes earned about £200 net per annum at
the start, but in time he acquired expensive living tastes and fat
fees from clients "increasingly sprinkled with royalty, nobility,
cabinet ministers, millionaires and foreign governments." Perhaps
Holmes expressed disdain for money because he had all he needed.

Michael Harrison's *In the Footsteps of Sherlock Holmes* (New
York, 1960) points out Holmes's "reluctance to consider — or even
discuss — money which is the universal and enduring neurosis of
the English middle-middle class." He goes on to say you can now
" 'place' Mr. Holmes...among the bourgeoisie with money enough
to get a sound education but with not quite enough money to
purchase a career in some established profession."

Now we have three points of view: 1) Holmes was not interested
in money, 2) he had enough, 3) he was too proud to discuss it
because he didn't have enough. If the last assumption was in his
mind he should have become aware while visiting this country that
many entrepreneurs were from poor to middle income families.

Really, Holmes must have been his own true self when he said
in "A Scandal in Bohemia": 'There's money in this case, Watson, if
there is nothing else." At any rate if aversion to money or lack of it
kept him out of business, we are not likely to know the truth of it.

Another influence may have been his early start as a consulting
detective, and thus the twig was bent. We see this in Justice of Peace
Trevor's remarks: "Mr. Holmes, but it seems to me that all the detectives of fact and of fancy would be children in your hands. That's
your line of life, sir, and you may take the word of a man who has
seen something of the world." These words were spoken in the
Master's first case "The Gloria Scott." They may have been the deci-
sive, lasting influence on his life.

But the thrill of being the master detective must have had a tremendous hold on Holmes — perhaps the greatest reason that can be
advanced for no change in his career in spite of his unexploited
talents for business. The uniqueness of choice is seen in "The

Speckled Band" where Dr. Watson reports: "working as he did rather for the love of his art than for the acquirement of wealth, he refused to associate himself with any investigation which did not tend towards the unusual, and even the fantastic."

In spite of all of these reasons why Holmes did not, would not, or could not enter life's arena as a business entrepreneur is the lurking suspicion that he had tried but could not continue for some reason. Or he felt frustrated because he had not given it a go. What else did this mean: "My mind is like a racing engine, tearing itself to pieces because it is not connected up with the work for which it was built"? ("Wisteria Lodge") Did he have flashes of self-revelation that pointed out how successful, how fulfilling it might have been if his choice had been that of a business entrepreneur?

In William S. Baring-Gould's chronology of the Master *(Sherlock Holmes of Baker Street,* New York 1962) he records Holmes commencing an eight months tour (1879) in America with the Sasanoff Shakespearean Company. While he was in the United States he became involved in "The Case of Vanderbilt and the Yeggman" ("The Adventure of the Sussex Vampire"). Was this not William Vanderbilt, the railroad tycoon?

Holmes traveled extensively in the United States. He must have read about, or seen, (or perhaps met through Vanderbilt) celebrated captains of industry and finance such as John D. Rockefeller, J. Pierpont Morgan, Andrew Carnegie, Philip D. Armour—and on and on. In them he must have recognized similar personality traits and abilities. Each of these had started on the lowest rung and came from poor families. The opportunity to see the great opportunities for entrepreneurs must have been there.

Into this speculation about Holmes's taking a quiet fling in business, actually or mentally, we cannot rule out what might have happened during the Great Hiatus (1891-1894) — from Reichenbach Fall to "The Adventure of the Empty House." Where was Holmes?

The theories on Holmes's whereabouts during the Great Hiatus proliferate. There are many who refuse to accept Holmes's explanation of his escape from the Napoleon of Crime, Moriarty, or his simple statement: "I traveled for two years in Tibet, therefore, and amused myself by visiting Lhassa, and spending some days with the head lama[5]. You may have read of the remarkable explorations of a

5. *The Strand Magazine* says Llama. Mr. Ogden Nash pointed out: The one-l lama. He's a priest, The two-l llama, He's a beast....ed.

Norwegian named Sigerson....I then passed through Persia, looked in at Mecca, and paid a short but interesting visit to the Khalifa at Khartoum....Returning to France I spent some months in a research into the coal-tar derivatives...." ("Empty House")

A fantasia had been composed by the inquisitive ranging from the skepticism that Holmes ever visited these places because he was in London all the time or visited the United States or was engaged in espionage elsewhere in the world or had gone off to marry Irene Adler. To compound the confusion there are those who believe one or more of these possibilities at Reichenbach Fall: both Moriarty and Holmes died, both survived, only Moriarty survived because he was Holmes or because he was not. To all of this implausibility one might add a theory that the incident at the Fall occurred not at all.[6]

This bizarre accounting gives license to add one more: an industrial syndicate in the U.S. hired Holmes to look for oil in Persia. We know he knew Vanderbilt in America. It is easy to believe that he also became acquainted with Rockefeller and other industrial giants who easily left their own fields of concentration to invest in other opportunities. There is ample history, too, about British-Dutch-American consortiums formed to find oil throughout the world. We must believe some of these had very secret and early starts.

H. G. Wells observed "...Persia had before the first world war been a happy hunting ground for European diplomats....Great oil resources had been discovered and the American oil interests pursued devious paths of instigation and support." The presence of oil was known in Persia to the ancients. Serious commercial exploration was going on in the latter part of the 19th century, and the first successful concession was granted not many years after Holmes's visit to Persia. It all neatly coincides.

Holmes's talents could readily be perceived by those international oil barons. What better cover could there be than to employ the world's greatest detective who would not be suspected of involvement in an industrial enterprise! This cartel would naturally be assisted by concerned governments, not only because of the industrial potential but because of military and political implications.

In *A Study in Scarlet* Watson ascribes to Sherlock Holmes these limits: "Knowledge of Geology—Practical, but limited; Knowledge

6. Our Sigerson, E. W. McDiarmid has discussed these theories in "Reichenbach and beyond." *The Baker Street Journal*, 1957 Christmas Annual.–Ed.

of Chemistry—Profound." Given his intellectual background, adeptness at disguise, and this technical efficiency as well as his disarming cover as a private detective he would be an ideal observer to assess secretly the feasibility to engage further in oil prospecting in Persia.

Professor Remsen Ten Eyck Schenck says in "Baker Street Fables" *(Baker Street Journal,* v.2, no.2, April 1952) that "...research work in chemistry done by thousands..." in coal-tar derivatives could be described as did Holmes in accounting for his stay in France. Precisely! Holmes is clever at this type of legitimate deception.

Of course we cannot rule out the possibility of a double cover plan, that is, a cover within a cover. All of this about oil may have been to disguise a truer interest in some industrial activity known only to Holmes and his sponsors.

So we have it. Holmes had all the attributes to be a business success. He was a latent, potential entrepreneur and may have regretted not making it a career instead of brief encounters with it. He would have discovered not only that the "game's afoot," but *that* game was *the* thing!

Who then would have been the world's greatest detective? That problem defies solution.

Joseph B. Connors

I

I WOULD like to propose a new solution to one of the oldest of Canonical problems. Perhaps it is *the* oldest problem, for Arthur Bartlett Maurice called attention to it as early as 1902.[1] I allude to the frequently discussed discrepancy between Watson's early report that when he quoted Thomas Carlyle, Holmes "inquired in the naïvest way who he might be and what he had done" and the subsequent exchange in *The Sign of the Four* after Holmes asks Watson if he is well up in his Jean Paul:

"Fairly so. I worked back to him through Carlyle."
"That was like following the brook to the parent lake."

If the solution I propose is correct, it will, as a by-product, provide "more data" for continuing investigation of another ancient Canonical problem, the often-settled, never-really-settled question of whether Holmes attended Oxford or Cambridge—or neither, or both.

It will not be necessary to dwell here on the wild inaccuracy of Watson's original appraisal of Holmes's knowledge of literature as *nil*, because Holmes's cosmopolitan literacy and his bibliophilism have been examined by many specialists. The suggestion occasionally encountered that Holmes "boned up" on previously neglected subjects after his early conversations with Watson can be summarily dismissed. Holmes's literary allusions have the flavor of a long and intimate acquaintance with literature. Besides, as Roger Lancelyn Green observes, it would have been foreign to Holmes's character to have tried to become as "multilegent" as possible by means of a crash program.[2]

The inescapable conclusion is that Holmes was deliberately misleading Watson when he asked him who Carlyle was. But why did he do so? In the early days of their acquaintance, before Watson even knew the nature of Holmes's profession, Holmes would hardly have indulged in a simple spoofing of Watson merely to satisfy an appetite for innocent merriment. It seems plain that both on this occasion and on the occasion when he professed ignorance of the

1. Edgar W. Smith, ed., *The Incunabular Sherlock Holmes* (Morristown, N.J., 1958), pp. 1-2.
2. Roger Lancelyn Green et al., "Knowledge of Literature—Nil?" *Sherlock Holmes Journal*, 2 (1973), 84.

solar system, he was adopting a particular conversational strategy. Gavin Brend is at least pointing in the right direction, I think, when he says that Holmes's query about Carlyle was probably made "at a time when Holmes wanted to give his whole attention to a case as yet unsolved, and simply could not be bothered to be drawn into a discussion about Carlyle or anything else."[3]

For whatever reason, Holmes at that point wanted to cut short any further discussion of Carlyle or quotation from him. As Brend observes, we do not know the circumstances under which the remark was made; nor, I would add, do we know the precise form it took. We do not know if Watson is quoting Holmes exactly when he says that he "inquired in the naïvest way" who Carlyle might be or what he had done. Did Holmes's query take the form of a blunt question, like Harold Ross's famous copyreading notation: "Who he?"? Or did a lazily smiling Holmes, after taking down his personal *Who's Who,* say something like "My field of vision has included Angus Carlyle, the Croydon coiner, and of course the unspeakable Malcolm Carlyle of Mile End Road, but your Carlyle has thus far escaped my notice"?

I suggest that Watson was in this instance the victim of a specific, classifiable rhetorical technique. I suggest, furthermore, that this technique was one at which men who had attended Oxford University were peculiarly adept. It was one ingredient of that complex, elusive, well-nigh indefinable mode of behavior that is sometimes called "the Oxford manner."

We may observe a striking illustration of the technique in the extraordinary debate between representatives of Oxford and Cambridge that took place at the Oxford Union on November 29, 1829, the result of a challenge issued by the Cambridge Union. A group of brilliant, earnest Cantabrigians — Arthur Henry Hallam, Thomas Sunderland, and Richard Monckton Milnes, later Lord Houghton — journeyed to Oxford to debate the question of whether Byron or Shelley was the greater poet. The Oxford debaters, who included Francis Doyle, later Oxford's Professor of Poetry, and Henry F. Manning, later Cardinal Manning, were to uphold the merits of Byron, who had received an M.A. at Cambridge. The Cambridge debaters were to support the supremacy of Shelley, who had been thrown out of Oxford (along with his closest friend, a youth with the Walt Disneyish name of Thomas Jefferson Hogg) as a conse-

3. Gavin Brend, *My Dear Holmes: a Study in Sherlock* (London, 1951), p.39.

quence of publishing a pamphlet entitled *The Necessity of Atheism.*[4]

Accounts of the debate in Victorian memoirs convey varying impressions of it. Manning, looking back on it across the years, remembered it as an utter rout of himself and the other Oxonians by the zealous, tempestuous Cambridge speakers. But that was not the way all the Cambridge delegates recalled it, as we learn from James Pope-Hennessy's *Monckton Milnes* (New York, 1955) I, 24:

> The debate was not, from the Cambridge viewpoint, quite the success that could have been wished....The Oxford young gentlemen seemed as elegant and unconcerned as their room, and lounged about the fireplace with provoking *sang-froid*. Worst of all, they alleged that they had never heard of Shelley, and one of them even pretended to think that the Cambridge contingent had come over to support the claims of Shenstone.

Do we not have here, among these early nineteenth-century Oxonians, a clear example of the type of gamesmanship (or upmanship) practiced by Holmes when he pretended that he had never heard of Carlyle?

Non-recognition of distinguished names was apparently characteristic of both town and gown at Oxford. When Thackeray stood unsuccessfully for Parliament for the City of Oxford in 1857, he had been famous for about a decade as the author of *Vanity Fair*. His opponent was Edward Cardwell, who had previously sat for Oxford for several years. Thackeray's first electioneering visit to the city was disconcerting. Later, meeting his opponent at the Athenaeum Club in London, he remarked, "Well, Cardwell, you know that I have been down among your damned constituents. Of course, I did not expect that all of them would have read my novels, but I certainly did expect that most of them would have heard of me; instead of which I found that the question on everyone's lips was 'Who the devil is Thackeray?' "[5]

When the young artist William Rothenstein visited Oxford in the summer term of 1893 to do portraits in lithograph of Oxford characters, one of his subjects was the learned critic Walter Pater, who had gone up to Oxford in 1858 and had been elected to a fellow-

4. Herbert Arthur Morrah, *The Oxford Union, 1823-1923* (London, 1923), pp.32-37.

5. C. Day Lewis and Charles Fenby, eds., *Anatomy of Oxford* (London, 1938), pp.42-43. The anecdote is quoted from G. C. Brodrick, *Memories and Impressions, 1831-1900* (London, 1900).

ship at Brasenose in 1864. One trait of Pater's particularly struck the artist. "He had a habit," he recalled, "disquieting to young people, of assuming ignorance on subjects about which he was perfectly informed."[6] Pater was an Oxford contemporary of the influential philosopher F. H. Bradley, fellow of Merton College. T. S. Eliot, a thorough student of Bradley's works, calls attention to "his habit of discomfiting an opponent with a sudden profession of ignorance" (though Eliot does attribute the habit to a genuine modesty on Bradley's part).[7]

Here is a more recent specimen, from Christopher Sykes' biography of a highly cultivated Oxonian, Evelyn Waugh. Sykes describes his attempts to persuade Waugh that he should allow film producers to go ahead with a film version of his novel *Brideshead Revisited*. The conversation went, in part, like this:

> Waugh: You have no notion of what these people might want to do to my book.
> Sykes: I have every notion. I have seen many films in my lifetime, and I have read Beachcomber's account of Sol Hogwasch's film entitled "The Life of Bach."
> Waugh: He was a musician, wasn't he?[8]

The fine art of feigning ignorance of a subject, either to mask an imperfect knowledge of it, or to lead a conversational antagonist into a trap, or, more commonly, to express disdain or boredom, is no doubt part of an ancient tradition, perhaps originally practiced by medieval Oxford clerks of a more guileful and supercilious breed than Chaucer's gentle Clerk of Oxenford. It was one of an array of weapons available to practitioners of the Oxford snub. C. Day Lewis and Charles Fenby, in their charming anthology *Anatomy of Oxford,* illustrate the Oxford snub with a curious reminiscence by Sir Richard Steele, a resident successively of Christ Church and of Merton College between 1689 and 1692. In *Tatler* No. 197 (July 5, 1710) Steele discusses the problem of dealing with a tiresome conversationalist:

> I remember, in my youth it was a humour at the University, when a fellow pretended to be more eloquent than ordinary...or triumph over us with an argument ...it was the humour to shut one eye....If amongst us on such an occasion each man offered a voluntary

6. William Rothenstein, *Men and Memories* (New York, 1931), I, p.139.

7. T. S. Eliot, "Francis Herbert Bradley," *Selected Essays, 1917-1932* (New York, 1932), pp.358-359.

8. Christopher Sykes, *Evelyn Waugh: a Biography* (Boston, 1975), p.300.

rhetorician some snuff, it would probably produce the
same effect. As the matter now stands, whether a man
will or no, he is obliged to be informed in whatever
another pleases to entertain him with....[9]

Steele's engaging vignette of seventeenth-century Oxford life
forecasts, I believe, the kind of situation which caused Watson to fall
victim to the particular form of social strategy I have been examin-
ing. Why was Watson quoting Carlyle? Was he, to use Steele's
terms, waxing more eloquent than ordinary at the breakfast table,
perhaps in response to a leader in the *Times*? (We know that even
in these early Baker Street days, Watson did not hesitate to be vehe-
ment, to judge by his explosive reaction to Holmes's article "The
Book of Life": "What ineffable twaddle!...I never read such rubbish
in my life.") Or had he exerted himself to triumph over his new
acquaintance with an argument, perhaps, as a clincher, reeling off
from memory a whole paragraph of *Sartor Resartus*? Or had he—
and this seems to me most likely—been informing Holmes about
some Carlyle-related matter whether Holmes would or no? It is not
easy to imagine Holmes closing one eye, though he may on this occasion have closed both, as he sometimes did. Perhaps, in lieu of a
snuff-box, he extended the Persian slipper as a kind of put-that-in-
your-pipe-and-smoke-it gesture. At any rate, we know that he
brought Watson up short by saying, in effect, "And who is Carlyle?"

II

My examination of this single detail of Holmes's behavior has
led me to consider whether or not one may observe other elements of
an "Oxford manner" in his conversation or in his way of handling
certain social situations. Surely Holmes himself, if confronted with
a problem such as the venerable Canonical Oxford-or-Cambridge
problem, would have arrived at a solution within a few minutes simply by close scrutiny of the person in question. Can anyone doubt
that Holmes, who could instantly identify a military man or a physician by his bearing and demeanor, would have readily exposed an
Oxonian masquerading for whatever reason as a Cantabrigian, or
vice versa, by applying his usual methods of observation?

In referring to the Oxford manner as something nearly indefinable, I have meant, of course, that one is not likely to come up with a
definition that is generally accepted. The term obviously means dif-

9. *Anatomy of Oxford*, p.46.

ferent things to different persons. I think, however, that almost anyone who has used the term would find in the following definition,
composed by Wallace Blair-Fish in 1925, at least a phrase or two
that he can approve:

> ...that defensive nonchalance, that non-enthusiasm
> (which are possibly the nearest one can get to what is
> meant by 'the Oxford manner')...To be cool, to be
> casual, to be contemptuous — in a word, emotionless,
> with the innate remove of a Brahmin or a Samurai:
> that is Oxford.[10]

Sherlock Holmes was an extraordinarily complex man (which is
why no stage or screen actor has ever been completely satisfactory in
the role); but in detail after detail, does not that definition remind
one of Holmes as Watson sometimes viewed him in the early days of
their association? Of the Holmes that much of the world saw much
of the time?

In Watson's very first opportunity to observe Holmes at work,
when the two arrived at Lauriston Gardens, he was struck by his
companion's unusually casual manner. "With an air of nonchalance,"
he recalls, "which, under the circumstances, seemed to me to border
upon affectation, he lounged up and down the pavement, and gazed
vacantly at the ground, the sky, the opposite houses and the line of
railings." Watson quickly had an opportunity to observe another
element of the Oxford manner in the coolly contemptuous irony with
which Holmes responded to Gregson's and Lestrade's fatuous comments on the case. When Gregson, describing the tremendous "strain
upon the mind" which he had been experiencing, said, "You will
appreciate that, Mr. Sherlock Holmes, for we are both brain-
workers." Holmes said gravely, "You do me too much honour." A
moment later, Gregson, crowing over the fact that he had visited the
firm that produced Drebber's hat and that Holmes had not, admonished him, "you should never neglect a chance, however small it may
seem." Holmes replied, "To a great mind, nothing is little."

In this same conversation we find, too, the first demonstration by
Holmes of another weapon in the Oxford armory: the calculated or
rhetorical yawn. Gregson was pouring forth his account of his inter-
view with Madame Charpentier:

> "At times she spoke so low that I could hardly catch
> the words. I made shorthand notes of all that she said,

10. Blair [pseud. of Wallace Blair-Fish], *Oxford Ways* (Oxford, 1925), p.69.

however, so that there should be no possibility of a mistake."

"It's quite exciting," said Sherlock Holmes, with a yawn. "What happened next?"

The Sherlockian yawn is another expression of 'that defensive nonchalance, that non-enthusiasm," and it has an obvious kinship with the technique of feigned ignorance. Holmes used it for a somewhat different purpose in "The Second Stain" after his hasty examination of the secret compartment beneath the carpet. When Lestrade returned to the room, he found Holmes "leaning languidly against the mantelpiece, resigned and patient, endeavoring to conceal his irrepressible yawns."

One would think that one of the most yawn-proof narratives on record is the account of the midnight moorland ride of Hugo Baskerville and his riotous companions. (What would any of us give to sit beside the Baker Street fireplace and listen to it for the first time?) But what is Holmes's immediate response to it? Holmes "yawned and tossed the end of his cigarette into the fire."

The most impressive demonstrations of Holmes's defensive nonchalance and cool, casual contempt occur in his conversations with persons who are pompous, arrogant, or menacing. Holmes has little respect for the King of Bohemia when he takes his case:

"...I have come incognito from Prague for the purpose of consulting you."

"Then, pray consult," said Holmes, shutting his eyes once more.

He has even less respect for him at the end of the case:

"What a woman — oh, what a woman! ...Is it not a pity that she was not on my level?"

"From what I have seen of the lady she seems indeed to be on a very different level to your majesty," said Holmes coldly.

Lord St. Simon ("The Noble Bachelor") makes the mistake of telling Holmes, "I understand that you have already managed several delicate cases of this sort, sir, though I presume that they were hardly from the same class of society." "No, I am descending," says Holmes. "...My last client of the sort was a king."

Holmes's rejoinders to Dr. Grimesby Roylott ("The Speckled Band") and to Neil Gibson ("Thor Bridge"), both of whom seem prepared to do him physical violence, are models of defensive nonchalance; in each instance, to use Holmes's own description of a

parallel type of encounter, it is a straight left against a slogging ruf-
fian. "It is a little cold for the time of the year," he tells the raging
Roylott. "But I have heard that the crocuses promise well." When
Gibson raised a huge, knotted fist, Holmes "smiled languidly,"
reached for his pipe, and admonished the Gold King: "Don't be
noisy, Mr. Gibson. I find that after breakfast even the smallest argument is unsettling. I suggest that a stroll in the morning air and a
little quiet thought will be greatly to your advantage." In diction,
in structure, in tone, is that not an Oxonian utterance?

I suspect that a close comparative study of (a) Holmes's rhetoric
throughout the entire Canon and (b) the rhetoric of selected distinguished Oxford graduates of the 1860's and 1870's might be most
illuminating. I am convinced, for example, that the famous *sherlockismus,* singled out for commentary by Ronald Knox in 1910, was a
product of mid-Victorian Oxford life, though the fact that Knox, an
Oxford man himself, did not recognize it as such shows that like
many such catchy linguistic structures, it had only a temporary
vogue. The so-called *sherlockismus* was also employed by Oscar
Wilde, whose Oxford career spanned the years 1874-1878 (the years
immediately following, or slightly overlapping, the period desig-
nated by several biographers of Holmes as the period of his university experience). Consider first the structure of the two classical
examples of the *sherlockismus* cited by Knox, in each of which a
paradox is produced by turning something negative into something
emphatically positive:

"Is there any other point to which you would wish to
draw my attention?"
"To the curious incident of the dog in the night-time."
"The dog did nothing in the night-time."
"That was the curious incident."

*   *   *

"How do you know that?"
"I followed you."
"I saw no one."
"That is what you may expect to see when I follow
you."

Consider next two anecdotes narrated in H. Montgomery Hyde's
Oscar Wilde (New York, 1975), pp. 136-137, 158. In the first of
these, Wilde is in conversation with Beerbohm Tree, after the first
performance of *A Woman of No Importance:*

Wilde: I shall always regard you as the best critic of
my plays.

Tree: But I have never criticized your plays.

Wilde: That's why.

In the second, Wilde is complaining to Richard Le Gallienne shortly
after the publication of the latter's book *The Religion of a Literary
Man:*

Wilde: Well, you were very unkind to me in that book
—most unkind....

Le Gallienne: Why, Oscar, I don't know what you
mean by being unkind to you....I can't remember that
I even mentioned your name in it.

Wilde: Ah, Richard. That was just it!

What we see here, in two men of radically different tempera-
ments, may be the lingering influence, perhaps the indirect influence,
of some long-forgotten, witty mid-Victorian don: the echo of a single
engaging passage in a lecture, a conversation, even a sermon—the
kind of verbal gem that is quoted and widely imitated (just as the
Reverend W. A. Spooner's "Kinquering Kongs Their Titles Take"
spawned a whole school of Spoonerisms).

Perhaps this same witty don that I have envisaged was also responsible for a bit of sardonic analysis of the way of the world that
stuck in the mind of more than one undergraduate. "What you do
in this world is of no consequence," says Holmes at the conclusion of
A Study in Scarlet. "The question is, what can you make people
believe that you have done?" And Wilde, commenting on the false
report that he had actually "walked down Piccadilly with a poppy or
a lily in his medieval hand," observed, "Anyone could have done that.
The difficult thing was to make people believe that I had done it."

N. P. Metcalfe, Baring-Gould, and other students of the subject
who share their views may well be right in arguing that Holmes
attended both Oxford and Cambridge. But, though I grant that the
evidence I have submitted here is merely suggestive rather than con-
clusive, there is no doubt in my own mind as to which university left
its unmistakable stamp on him. I am convinced that if some contemporary of Holmes had been endowed with the Master's own gifts, he
might have remarked, after observing Holmes closely, "Beyond the
obvious facts that he works frequently with chemicals, that he plays
the violin, that he has done some boxing, and that he has spent some
time at Oxford, I can determine very little."

HOLMES, WATSON, AND WINE
John E. Bergquist

ALTHOUGH the British have never enjoyed an international reputation as connoisseurs of food and fine wines, the Canon yields many references which show that Sherlock Holmes and Dr. Watson were atypical Englishmen in this respect. Unlike many of their countrymen, who were more comfortable ingesting porter, stout, or ale as accompaniments to Scotch eggs and steak-and-kidney-pie, Holmes and Watson were often found enjoying the fruit of the vine as a complement to more Epicurean fare.

In *The Sign of the Four,* Holmes, Watson, and Athelney Jones of Scotland Yard sat down in the Baker Street rooms to "oysters and a brace of grouse, with something a little choice in white wines." Afterwards, they relaxed over port before embarking on the Thames River chase in pursuit of Jonathan Small and the Andaman Islander, Tonga. In the same adventure Watson mentioned that he had taken Beaune[1] with his lunch, which gave him the courage to chastise Holmes for his use of cocaine.

The elegant cold supper which Holmes had catered at 221B for Lord Robert St. Simon (who declined to partake), Hatty Doran, and Francis Hay Moulton in "The Adventure of the Nobel Bachelor," included "a group of ancient and cobwebby bottles."

Port is again mentioned in "The Adventure of the Creeping Man," when Holmes remembered that there was "an inn (in Camford) called the Chequers where the port used to be above mediocrity and the linen was above reproach," and in "The Gloria Scott," when Holmes recalled that he, Victor Trevor, and Trevor senior had sat "over a glass of port after dinner" at Donnithorpe.

In "The Cardboard Box," Holmes and Watson "had a pleasant little meal together" at a hotel in Wallington; afterwards they "sat for an hour over a bottle of claret"[2] while Holmes regaled Watson with "anecdote after anecdote" about the virtuoso violinist

1. By "Beaune," Watson was probably referring to one of many medium-priced wines of the Côte de Beaune region in Burgundy, rather than one actually bearing the Hospice de Beaune label. The cost of the latter would have been prohibitive at this time to "an army surgeon with a weak leg (or shoulder?) and a weaker banking account" (*The Sign of the Four*).

2. "Claret" is an Anglicized form of the old French *clairet,* a pale red wine initially imported from France in the twelfth century. The term now (and in Holmes and Watson's day) refers to any good red Bordeaux.

Paganini.[3] Holmes apparently had an especial fondness for claret, for he chose it to break his self-imposed fast in "The Dying Detective," saying, "I never needed it more."

The most elegant wine mentioned in the Canon is Montrachet, "the greatest of the White Burgundies. ...A good bottle of Montrachet is an experience no one who drinks it can forget."[4] It is puzzling why Holmes referred to such a wine so casually: "There is a cold partridge on the sideboard, Watson, and a bottle of Montrachet. Let us renew our energies before we make a fresh call upon them" ("The Veiled Lodger"). Since "The Veiled Lodger" occurred late in 1896, approximately a year after "The Bruce-Partington Plans," the Montrachet could have been an additional token of appreciation from Queen Victoria (along with the "remarkably fine emerald tie-pin") for Holmes's services to the British government in the latter case. Holmes, in character, would then have treated the prize off-handedly,[5] rather than saving it for a special occasion as one would expect. If this assumption is correct, it is also possible that the proud Holmes was miffed that Her Majesty had not bothered to ascertain his tastes in wine, and instead presented him with a bottle of good claret, such as Château Margaux or Château Lafite-Rothschild.

I must mention in passing that the reference to Beaune and Montrachet point out an error by the eminent Holmesian scholar Michael Harrison, who states that claret is the only French wine mentioned by name in the saga.[6]

The last canonical reference, chronologically speaking, to wine-bibbing is found in "His Last Bow," when Holmes and Watson, after having chloroformed Von Bork, helped themselves to the German spy's Imperial Tokay, secured from "Franz Josef's special cellar at the Schoenbrunn Palace." Holmes then demonstrated his appreciation of fine wine by asking Watson, "Might I trouble you to open the window, for chloroform vapour does not help the palate."

As to their usual sources of wine, when Holmes and Watson were in residence at No. 221B, they most likely would have patronized the wine-merchant's shop at No. 16, Baker Street, (almost directly across the street), belonging to H. Dolamore & Co.[7] Holmes may also have

3. Undoubtedly among the anecdotes was the legend that Paganini had sold his soul to the devil in exchange for the gift of awesome instrumental technique.

4. John Storm, *An Invitation to Wines*, New York, 1955.

5. Is this another example of the Oxford manner discussed by Mr. Connors? –Ed.

6. Michael Harrison, *In the Footsteps of Sherlock Holmes*, New York, 1972.

7. *Ibid.*

kept up a relationship with "Vamberry, the wine merchant" ("The Musgrave Ritual");[8] perhaps Vamberry offered Holmes a perennial discount as a *quid pro quo* for Holmes's invaluable assistance in clearing up a problem.

Although James Windibank ("A Case of Identity") was a traveller in wines "for Westhouse & Marbank, the great claret importers of Fenchurch Street," it is highly unlikely that Holmes ever did any business with him after their encounter, as he referred to Windibank as "a cold-blooded scoundrel," and said of him, "there never was a man who deserved punishment more." Upon making these remarks in the Baker Street rooms at the conclusion of the case, Holmes moved as if to carry out said punishment himself with a hunting crop. Windibank then dashed to the door, clattered down the stairs, and ran "at the top of his speed down the road." We can safely assume that the two never met again.

In addition to the previously cited instances, there are several other allusions to wine in the saga. Thaddeus Sholto offered Mary Morstan her choice of a glass of Chianti or Tokay, saying that he kept no other wines *(The Sign of the Four)*. (Miss Morstan refused the offer—she may have been trying to impress Dr. Watson, as a prospective suitor, with her sense of propriety.) In "The Gloria Scott," Trevor senior stated in his written narrative of the shipboard mutiny that a convict named Wilson, upon breaking in a locker in the "Gloria Scott's" stateroom, "pulled out a dozen of brown sherry." The mutineers then "cracked off the necks of the bottles, poured the stuff out into tumblers, and (tossed them off)." (This is undoubtedly the crudest episode of wine-drinking mentioned in the Sacred Writings, but one must keep the circumstances in mind.) Another second-hand allusion to wine was made by the anonymous narrator of Part 2 of *The Valley of Fear;* Bodymaster McGinty, Birdy Edwards (in his role as Jack McMurdo), and Ted Baldwin toasted the brotherhood of the Scowrers with champagne.[9]

8. It would be interesting to find out if this Vamberry was related to the Hungarian professor Arminium Vambery (sic), who provided Bram Stoker (a London contemporary of Holmes and Watson) with information on Dracula and vampire legends. Stoker incorporated this information into his novel, *Dracula.* (Raymond T. McNally and Radu Florescu, *In Search of Dracula,* New York, 1972). If so, Vamberry was probably also a Hungarian, and it is likely that he would have specialized in Tokay.

9. They probably drank a New York State champagne, due to the proximity of the New York wine region to "Vermissa Valley." The bottle may well have borne the Great Western label, as that is the oldest vintage in that area. Great Western's "claim to fame is a champagne that has won awards in European competitions." (Fadiman & Aaron, *Wine Buyers Guide,* New York, 1977.)

More importantly, there were wine-related clues which helped Holmes solve two of his cases. In "The Abbey Grange," from observing that only one of the three wineglasses found at the scene of the crime contained beeswing,[10] Holmes correctly deduced "That only two glasses were used, and that the dregs of both were poured into a third glass, so as to give the false impression that three people had been (there)." This led to the further deductions that Lady Brackenstall and her maid were not telling the truth regarding the circumstances surrounding the death of Sir Eustace, and that they were covering up for the true killer. Combining this information with that obtained through other observations and deductions, Holmes quickly solved the case.

In "The Noble Bachelor," Holmes was able to deduce that "F.H.M." had been a guest "at one of the most select London hotels" by the "select prices" indicated on his hotel bill. Among other charges on the bill was "glass sherry, 8d." This deduction helped Holmes to easily trace his quarry.

Brandy (basically, distilled wine, and an ingredient in fortified wines such as port and sherry), is given numerous mentions in the Canon, but almost exclusively as a restorative. Among other instances, Holmes and Watson gave brandy to Victor Hatherley after his harrowing experience, ("The Engineer's Thumb"), and to the prostrate Thorneycroft Huxtable, M.A., Ph.D., etc. ("The Priory School") as he lay "insensible upon (their) bearskin hearthrug." Watson himself was a recipient of this treatment after he fainted upon realizing that Holmes had seemingly returned from the dead ("The Empty House").

This profusion of cited references to the grape in the Sherlockian Canon shows without a doubt that both Holmes and Watson were familiar with various wines, and enjoyed consuming them. For example, one can easily imagine that on "a blazing hot day in August... (when) Baker Street was like an oven" (The Cardboard Box"),[11]

10. The beeswing suggests that the wine drunk by Lady Brackenstall and her lover was probably a crusted port, a rare and costly wine. If such a wine is handled gently one should be able to decant it without transferring any of the crust to the glasses, but, as Holmes observed, it took Captain Crocker three tries before he could remove the cork with his pocket corkscrew. This agitation undoubtedly caused the crust to leave the sides of the bottle, and to thus cloud the wine to such an extent that Holmes observed that "the bottle was full of (beeswing)."

11. Or on "a close, rainy day in October (with a) thermometer of 90" ("The Resident Patient"). See the discussion of these two passages in Trevor Hall, *Sherlock Holmes—Ten Literary Studies*, New York 1969.

Holmes or Watson could have walked to the sideboard, half-filled a tumbler with any of a number of wines from their private stock, added ice and charged water (from the gasogene), and enjoyed a Victorian version of the wine cooler. How did each man come to acquire this varied and cultivated taste for wines?

In the case of Holmes, if we are to accept Baring-Gould's[12] version of early events in the detective's life, the Holmes family journeyed widely throughout Europe during Sherlock's childhood. Among other places, their travels took them to Bordeaux, and to Cologne (near the German Rhine wine region). Even at such a young age, the precocious boy was likely to have picked up some of the wine lore of the Continent. Holmes's familial "French connection" is also relevant here; his grandmother "was the sister of Vernet, the French artist" ("The Greek Interpreter"). There also was apparently a German branch of the Vernet family, the Verners, as a Dr. Verner, "a distant relative of Holmes," bought Watson's Kensington practice with Holmes's financial assistance ("The Norwood Builder"). Thus Holmes, through contact with his relatives on the Continent, was likely to have been familiar with the wines of their native countries. The English Holmeses probably had their own wine-related traditions as well; in "The Greek Interpreter," Sherlock Holmes tells Watson, "My ancestors were country squires, who appear to have led much the same life as is natural to their class." We may assume that this lifestyle included the enjoyment of wine.

We know from "The Gloria Scott" and "The Musgrave Ritual" that Holmes was a college man — the writer refuses to touch the controversy over which university Holmes attended[13] — and that he had acquaintance there with scions of the moneyed, landed class such as Victor Trevor and Reginald Musgrave. Such men would have been thoroughly familiar with the joys of wine, and would have shared this knowledge with Holmes. (Indeed, we have already seen that Holmes was served port at the Trevor estate.)

Watson's antecedents also clearly point to the gentry. We know that as a lad he had attended school with Percy "Tadpole" Phelps, whose "mother's brother was Lord Holdhurst, the great conservative politician" ("The Naval Treaty"). Watson had played Rugby for Blackheath ("The Sussex Vampire"), and if that was his home

12. William S. Baring-Gould, *Sherlock Holmes of Baker Street,* New York, 1962.

13. Though Mr. Bergquist is unwilling to touch the controversy we are quite prepared to accept Professor Connors' decision) –Ed.

neighborhood, he probably grew up in at least an upper-middle-class environment. After he had finished his preliminary education, he "took (his) degree of Doctor of Medicine at the University of London" *(A Study in Scarlet)*. John's eldest brother had been "left with good prospects" upon the death of their father *(The Sign of the Four)*. Such a milieu certainly would have included wine.[14]

Watson claimed to have "an experience of women which (extended) over many nations and three separate continents" *(The Sign of the Four)*.[15] Wine had undoubtedly played a part in some of these amorous experiences.

The clincher which proves beyond a reasonable doubt that Watson knew his wine is found in "The Stock-broker's Clerk." In that adventure, Watson likens Holmes's satisfaction at having had a worthy problem presented to him to that of "a connoisseur who has just taken his first sip of a comet vintage." (A comet wine is one from a vintage year in which a comet appeared, and according to wine lore therefore supposed to be of exceptional quality.)

Having laid the groundwork for Watson's interest in wine, the writer will now attempt to prove by circumstantial evidence that Dr. John H. Watson was actually a partner in a California winery! For documentation we must look to two non-canonical sources regarding events in Watson's life.

First, if we again turn to Baring-Gould,[16] we find that Watson journeyed to San Francisco in 1884 to tend to his sick brother. While there he "bought a (medical) practice, (and) met and wooed Miss Constance Adams of that city." (Baring-Gould alleges that Miss Adams became the first Mrs. Watson.) Watson then returned to London in late 1886.

During this period the California wine industry was undergoing remarkable expansion. "Between 1877 and 1895 (annual) produc-

14. I trust that wine in the home was not what sent the eldest brother on the road to an early death after having taken to drink *(The Sign of the Four)*.

15. The three continents would have been Europe (obviously), Asia, i.e., Afghanistan and the Indian subcontinent *(A Study in Scarlet)*, and North America (this assertion will be taken up presently). Although in *The Sign of the Four*, Watson told Mary Morstan and Holmes that he had been near Ballarat (in Australia), he had probably only been a young boy at the time, and not yet preoccupied with the opposite sex.

16. Baring-Gould, *op. cit.* See also the comments on *Angels of Darkness* in John Dickson Carr, *The Life of Sir Arthur Conan Doyle*, New York, 1949, and "Dr. Watson's Marriages" in Trevor Hall, *The Late Mr. Sherlock Holmes and Other Literary Studies*, New York, 1971.

tion jumped from 4,000,000 gallons to 17,000,000 gallons."[17] Surely a wine-lover such at Watson would have been aware of all this activity going on around him, and, being in need of funds, he may even have pondered on the financial gain possible for one who was able to "get in on the ground floor" of the fledgling boom industry.

Our second non-canonical clue concerning Watson's "California connection" comes from a series of radio broadcasts over the Mutual Broadcasting System in the mid-1940's.[18] In this series, sponsored by the *Petri Wine Company* of San Francisco, California, we find that Dr. Watson has retired to a *"Northern California* bungalow!" (Emphasis mine.)

It is this writer's assertion that Watson had been a stockholder in the Petri Wine Company, and that he retired to California to better look after his business interests. His involvement probably came about through treating a member of the Petri family at his San Francisco practice; cash was scarce, and in lieu of paying their bill the Petris offered Watson shares in their winery, which he readily accepted. The Petris may even have felt that it was to their advantage to have an Englishman as a partner at this time, because the California vintners were trying to develop "a modest export trade. There were tentative, if not sensationally successful, efforts to break into the European market."[19]

Watson sold his practice and returned to England when he was more financially secure. For several years he probably thought little about his stock holdings. However, the Petri family "took time to (make) good wine."[20] The business prospered, becoming "the proudest name in the history of American wine."[21] Watson's stock became very valuable, and he found himself with an independent source of income.

This additional revenue explains how Watson could often afford a household containing servants, when he usually devoted little time to his practice (if he kept one at all), and spent "about half (his) wound pension" on horse racing ("Shoscombe Old Place"). By 1902

17. Philip M. Wagner, *American Wines and Wine-Making,* New York, 1965.

18. Stories in this series were written by Denis Green and Anthony Boucher. Nigel Bruce played Watson in a dual role as narrator and as a participant in the adventures; Basil Rathbone portrayed Holmes. The announcer was Harry Bartell.

19. Wagner, *op. cit.*

20. Harry Bartell, in the Mutual Broadcasting System series.

21. *Ibid.*

he was even prosperous enough to have rooms in Queen Anne Street ("The Illustrious Client").

Like so many formerly family-owned businesses, the Petri Wine Company, although the label still exists, has since been absorbed into a huge corporation, by way of a succession of moves. It apparently first became part of Italian Swiss Colony of California, but Louis Petri gained control of the parent firm and produced good results; the noted wine expert Alexis Lichine states, "When Louis Petri ran Italian Swiss Colony from the 1940's to the late 1960's, the winery organization became one of the largest in the world."[22] United Vintners, Inc., which also owns the Inglenook and Beaulieu vineyards in California, then acquired Italian Swiss Colony. The final step was the acquisition of United Vintners, Inc., by Heublein, Inc., a food and beverage conglomerate with 1977 sales of over $1.5 billion.[23]

If the Petri family is no longer involved in the operation of its erstwhile winery, what of Watson and his heirs? I would like to think that somewhere in Northern California there still lives a very old Englishman who, as he sits and rocks on his patio on a summer evening, beams with pride to know that the present Chairman and Chief Executive Officer of Heublein, Inc., is one S. D. Watson![24]

So we leave the good Doctor comfortably ensconced in his bungalow, likely enjoying a glass of Petri port as he watches the sunset. And what of Holmes and wine in *his* latter years? Since he was an amateur chemist as well as a connoisseur of wines, it is easy to understand why beekeeping interested him so. One can imagine him even now in his cottage upon the Sussex Downs, calling out from his study, "Come, Martha, and share the sunset with me. Oh, and please bring us each a glass of mead, would you?"

22. Alexis Lichine's *New Encyclopedia of Wines & Spirits,* New York, 1977.

23. Standard & Poor's *Corporation Records,* 1977. Among other things Heublein, Inc., owns Kentucky Fried Chicken!

24. *Ibid.*

THE MASTER AND THE MAESTRO
Some Influences of Sherlock Holmes on Ellery Queen
J. Randolph Cox B.S.I.

No WRITER works in a vacuum. Even the most formula-prone will be influenced by outside forces, and by those who came before. Just as Conan Doyle owed a debt to Edgar Alan Poe and Gaboriau, almost every mystery writer since 1887 owes something to Sherlock Holmes. Ellery Queen, the writer, consciously emulated S. S. Van Dine in his early novels, but spiritually he also followed the Master.

It was in a review of an early Queen novel by the London *Times* that the phrase "the logical successor to Sherlock Holmes" was first used. It was reprinted as a dust jacket and paperback blurb on the Ellery Queen books for years before being replaced by Anthony Boucher's remark that "Ellery Queen *is* the American detective story." But a reviewer's phrase isn't enough to link the character of Ellery Queen (whom Sgt. Velie refers to as "The Maestro") with the man we have come to call the Master. There must be more than that.

Ellery Queen's interest in and admiration for Sherlock Holmes can be demonstrated easily enough. Frederic Dannay (one half of the writing team known to the world as Ellery Queen) for many years has been a member of the Baker Street Irregulars. As editor, Ellery Queen in 1944 produced a famous anthology of Holmesian parodies and pastiches called *The Misadventures of Sherlock Holmes*. Part of the Introduction to this volume was an historical survey of the Holmesian imitators and the variant forms of the names Sherlock Holmes and Doctor Watson. The remainder of the Introduction was an autobiographical account by Dannay of his first encounter with Sherlock Holmes. This memoir reappeared in a number of places and fittingly so, for it is a vivid account of the manner in which Holmes has appealed to the young. A revised version of the historical-bibliographical section was used as the Introduction to the first edition of August Derleth's *The Memoirs of Solar Pons* (1951).

There is ample evidence in the pages of *Ellery Queen's Mystery Magazine* to add to these references. For years EQMM has published its share of Sherlockiana, often in the issues which have appeared in time to be placed at each member's plate at the January dinner of The Baker Street Irregulars. Most of these contributions have been in the form of parodies or pastiches, but there have been a few scholarly articles as well.

But what of the Ellery Queen canon itself? Is there evidence there of Sherlockian influences on story structure, on character, on incident? How does the Queen's Universe resemble the Holmesian World?

The resemblance is greatest in the early Queen stories. Where Holmes emphasizes the importance of observation and the science of deduction, Ellery stresses observation and analytical logic. Again and again we see Ellery's faith in logic — in simple equations which solve the most complex problems. But there are differences as well and thus we often get only an echo of Holmes and not a slavish imitation. It is as though Holmes (or his shadow) were looking over the American detective's shoulder and guiding him in subtle ways.

The apartment on West 87th Street which Ellery shares with his father is described in swift strokes in *The Roman Hat Mystery* (1929). There is the heavily-carpeted stair, the huge oaken door with the framed motto "The Queens." The famous and near-famous have passed through that door.

The foyer leading to the living-room has a tapestry depicting the chase, a gift of "the Duke of . . . ., that impulsive gentleman whose son Richard Queen had saved from a noisome scandal, the details of which have never been made public." The reference to famous clients whose names are disguised and a case for which the world is not yet prepared certainly echo the career of the Master.

In the Queens' living-room, bookcases cover three walls with a large fireplace on the fourth wall. Over the solid oak beam mantel are "the famous crossed sabres, a gift from the old fencing-master of Nuremburg with whom Richard had lived in his younger days during his studies in Germany." The European emphasis may reflect more Van Dine than Doyle, but the symbol of a trophy of a past adventure has the Holmesian touch.

While the furnishings ("easy-chairs, armchairs, low divans, footstools, bright-colored leather cushions") seem more ostentatious than those at Baker Street, we must remember we are 1,000 miles from London and three decades later. A final touch is the introduction of Djuna, "man-of-all-work, general factotum, errand boy, valet, and mascot…picked up by Richard Queen during the period of Ellery's studies at college, when the old man was very much alone." Here is another tantalizing glimpse of the past, somewhat related to those we have of Holmes in "The Musgrave Ritual" or "The Greek Interpreter." (Somewhat later, in one of the short stories, we learn that Ellery's college was Harvard.)

Perhaps the richest source of Holmesian echoes in the Queen canon is the first collection of short stories, *The Adventures of Ellery Queen* (1934). Not only is the book title properly Holmesian, but each story-title has the same Holmesian prefix, "The Adventure of." Nearly every story embodies some theme or concept from the Holmes saga.

In "A Scandal in Bohemia" Holmes explains to Watson the distinction between seeing the steps which lead up from the hall to his rooms and observing them enough to know how many there are. "You see, but you do not observe....Now, I know that there are seventeen steps, because I have both seen and observed." In Ellery Queen's "The Adventure of the African Traveler," the importance of observation is demonstrated to a class in Applied Criminology:

A cracked watch crystal, with the watch stopped at 10:20, can be an indicator of the time of death, if only it is interpreted correctly;

A crease in the watch strap is at the second hole, but there is another and deeper crease at the third, an indication that the watch has once been worn on a smaller wrist;

Talcum powder on a dead man's face has been put on smoothly, probably with a brush, but no brush is found...immediately.

All these, and more, point to a murderer if only one is observant enough.

In "The Adventure of the Hanging Acrobat" we find a demonstration of the Holmesian principle that when you have eliminated the impossible, whatever remains, however improbable, must be the truth. Hanging was not the best or most convenient method of murdering Myra Brinkerhof, yet hanged she was. There must be a reason. Finding the reason also finds the killer.

In "The Adventure of the One-Penny Black" we find a number of Holmesian allusions. Mr. Uneker, the bookseller, has customers who have been robbed of their copies of *Europe in Chaos*. He knows about Ellery from newspaper accounts. ("I hear of Sherlock everywhere...") The thefts from the very shelves of the book purchasers have a Holmesian ring. Remember "The Adventure of the Six Napoleons" in which someone tracks down and smashes all the busts of Napoleon sold from one particular shop? "The One-Penny Black" is a rare postage stamp, stolen earlier from Friedrich Ulm, stamp dealer. The thief, it would seem, has done with the postage stamp what Beppo does with the black pearl of the Borgias and hidden it in one of the books. When the books are sold, he traces the purchasers in search of the right copy. Or is it that simple? In Ellery Queen's world the truth is often deeper than one at first imagines.

There are elements of Holmesian logic in "The Adventure of the Bearded Lady," but other influences are perhaps too subtle to go into here. To discuss them in depth would reveal more of the story than one should—especially for anyone who has not yet read it. However, it will be revealing little if we mention the use of the smoke bomb ruse which enables Ellery to search one of the rooms in the house. This ancient device—a reversal of that used by Holmes in "A Scandal in Bohemia"—actually has its origins in Poe's "The Purloined Letter." In that instance, you will recall, Dupin used it to make Minister D . . . . reveal the hiding place of the famous and incriminating letter.

It would be altogether too neat if particular Holmesian influences could be found in each of the eleven stories in *The Adventures of Ellery Queen*. The Holmesian sense is a spiritual rather than a corporeal one in "The Adventure of the Three Lame Men." While the title suggests one of those unrecorded adventures Dr. Watson was so fond of mentioning, there is little else that need concern us now.

Holmesian and Queenian logic blend in a passage like this from "The Adventure of the Invisible Lover"

> "Then, since his automatic was used, it logically follows that—granted he's telling the truth—some one stole it from him and replaced it secretly after the murder?"

And what of this Holmesian posture?

> "Frowning, [Ellery] got to his feet and began to prowl. He prowled the length and breadth of the room, stooped over like an old hunchback, his underlip thrust forward and his eyes straining. He even sprawled full length on the floor to grope beneath pieces of furniture; and he made a tour under the bed like a sapper in No Man's Land."

Certainly an echo of that famous example from *A Study in Scarlet* when the Master scrutinized walls and floor with his magnifying glass. When asked by Iris Scott if he has found out anything, Holmes's "We progress, my dear Watson, we progress" from "The Missing Three-Quarter" surely can be heard as Ellery says "I think I may tell you that young Lothario faces a rosier prospect than he faced this morning. Yes, yes, we have made strides."

So many detectives in literature have found illegalities a necessity at some point in a case that Holmes's famed "commuting a felony" in "The Adventure of the Blue Carbuncle" has much company if it serves as an influence here. So we pass over Ellery's hasty (and illegal) exhuming of the corpse with barely a mention.

The Sherlockian atmosphere of the opening passages of "The Adventure of the Teakwood Case" must be mentioned, however.

> The woody, leathery, homely living room of the Queens' apartment on West Eighty-seventh Street in New York City had seen queerer visitors than Mr. Seaman Carter, but surely none quite so ill at ease.

There is also a Holmesian ring to these opening lines from another story:

> Of all the hundreds of criminal cases in the solution of which Mr. Ellery Queen participated by virtue of his self-imposed authority as son of the famous Inspector Queen of the New York Detective Bureau, he has steadfastly maintained that none offered a simpler diagnosis than the case which he has designated as "The Adventure of the Glass-Domed Clock."

This story, incidentally, may feature the first use of a particularly Queenian convention, the dying clue.

One of the most often quoted passages from the Holmes canon is that about the dog in the night time. Inspector Gregory asks "Is there any other point to which you would wish to draw my attention?" Holmes replies, "To the curious incident of the dog in the night-time." Gregory says, "The dog did nothing in the night-time." "That (replies Holmes) was the curious incident." This device of the animal who does not bark and therefore shows an intruder to be familiar with the terrain is found throughout the literature of detection. A variation may be found in Ellery Queen's "The Adventure of the Two-Headed Dog." In that story also, the wait in the dark in the haunted room reminds us of those vigils in "The Speckled Band" and "The Red-Headed League."

Holmes frequently remarks on the extreme singularity of a case. In this same story Ellery says that "It was simple enough. But queer; damnably queer. I can't recall a queerer case."

Holmes was the author of several monographs on a variety of subjects such as tobacco and the Polyphonic Motets of Lassus. Ellery

Queen's literary contributions are, of course, the accounts of his own cases, but he assures us on concluding this case that someday he will write "a monograph on the phenomenon of coincidence."

And in "The Adventure of the Mad Tea Party" there is the reference to yesterday in the Holmesian manner. "How are you, Queen?" asks Paul Gardner, "I haven't seen you since I testified for your father in that Schultz murder case in the Village."

And if not hearing something that should be there can be significant (as in the dog in the night time), so is not *seeing* something that should be there. When Ellery looks into the room and does not see a clock reflected in a mirror is it the clock that is missing or the mirror? Is this a clock-in-the-night-time affair to match the Holmes incident?

These samples from the early Queen canon should suggest just how deep is his debt to Sherlock Holmes. There is a theory that the young Ellery Queen actually visited England and paid a call on his spiritual mentor. But just as any child grows to maturity and forsakes many of his early enthusiasms and influences, so the writer and the detective-hero have gone beyond Baker Street. Even in the early stories the emulation was not a slavish one, but by the 1940s there was a definite departure from the original theme. From a piece of Americana like *Calamity Town*, a psychological study like *Cat of Many Tails*, to the plea for simple justice in *The Glass Village* or the religious symbolism and hope of *And on the Eighth Day*, we can see a new Ellery Queen. He may have begun as "the logical successor to Sherlock Holmes," but he has continued as a logical contender for the broader title of the American Detective.

J. Randolph
Cox, B.S.I.

THE CASE
OF THE MISSING ZINCOGRAPHER
Ruth Berman

IN 1885, Lewis Carroll decided to have a facsimile edition published of the original manuscript of *Alice in Wonderland, Alice's Adventures Under Ground.* He met with various difficulties, and at one point even considered hiring a detective to trace an absconding zincographer. By a process of intricate deduction known as guesswork, it has been discovered that the detective he did not hire was Sherlock Holmes: I am indebted to Dean Dickensheet for some suggestions and criticisms in

"The Case of the Missing Zincographer"

It was in 1928 that Mr. Sherlock Holmes appeared at my door one morning and said that I was to accompany him to an auction at Sotheby's. It was true, I had no professional obligations to keep me. I had long since retired from practice. Nevertheless, his brusque invitation struck me as either frivolous or unreasonable, the more so as the day was cold and windy, with a light rain. However, I reflected that it was not like Holmes to be frivolous, and he was unreasonable only over matters of urgency.

I put on my coat and muffler, opened my umbrella, and marched out into the wind, expecting to hear a tale of crime—perhaps we were to prevent a robbery at Sotheby's? — but Holmes said nothing. We strode silently through the streets, our umbrellas tilted against the wind, to the omnibus stand. There was no queue, and we took our places by the kerb. Still he said nothing, but stood musing. At length I remarked, "What do you hope to find? a set of egg-shell pottery from the Ming dynasty?"

"I fear that would be beyond my purse," he said wryly. "Indeed, what I hope to see will be also too dear for me. It will be worth seeing, however. The manuscript of *Alice in Wonderland* is to be sold."

"Ah, I said, "your favorite text-book of pure logic."

"I told you in our first case together that the grand thing was to be able to reason backward. Where do you think I learned that if not in Looking-Glass Land?"

"Oh, yes," I said.

I tried to express only interest in my tone, but I fear that amusement must have been there as well. At any rate, Holmes glanced at me sharply and waited for me to say more.

"I was remembering how bashful you felt after you found out who he was."

"Was it so obvious?" he said ruefully.

"Not to him. He was too shy himself to see it."

Holmes said nothing. We stepped back, to avoid being splashed as the bus pulled in beside us, then hoisted ourselves onto the platform, and took seats inside.

*

In January of 1886 the Christmas spirit, or the cold, still inhibited the criminal population of London. Holmes had had no cases of interest in some weeks. Cases, indeed, had come to him, and he solved them, in many instances, without so much as leaving his chair. That morning, in particular, he sat through one sad and boring story after another, with only the consolations of his fee and his pipe. When I returned from my rounds at lunchtime the rooms ought to have been uninhabitable. I passed Lestrade coughing on the stair. Holmes, nevertheless, was still inside, ignoring the smoky fog he had created, and muttering to himself, something about Amy Robsart and the shocking degeneration of imagination in married men.

Cold and wet as it was outside, I flung open a window, and watched the smoke begin to coil outwards before I turned to the sideboard. There was cold beef there, happily. Holmes stared morosely while I hacked myself a slice. I cut off a second slice, flung it down by him, and ordered him to take some nourishment.

By the time we had finished these, we were both in better spirits. I was beginning to wonder if I wanted a sweet, enough to go hunting for the biscuit-tin, when Billy entered, followed by an elderly gentleman, as tall and thin as Holmes himself, but with a round — almost childlike — sweetness of expression.

"The reverend Mr. Dodgson, sir," Billy said.

I was surprised at the title, for he was not dressed like a parson, but then realized he was probably a Fellow at a college.

"M-mister Holmes?" said our visitor.

Holmes bowed, without rising. "Won't you be seated, Mr. Dodgson?" He nodded at me. "My associate, Dr. Watson."

Dodgson perched himself on the edge of a chair. "I have so l-little time at p-p — just now," he said apologetically. "Mr. M-macmillan is expecting me, but having made up my mind I should at least consult someone, and thinking I could at any rate describe my p—" He hesitated over what was no doubt to be "problem."

"You are an amateur photographer, I see," Holmes said.

"Yes. How—?"

"The odor of the chemicals lingers. Faint, but distinctive."

"Are you a student of photography, too, sir?" said Mr. Dodgson eagerly, losing his stammer. "I suppose as a detective you must find it highly useful."

"No," Holmes admitted, "I have not mastered the skills it requires. It is a difficult art. You are correct, however; it would be useful. If it becomes easier—"

"Oh, but the difficulty is half the charm! Indeed, it has become easier of late. Have you tried the new dry emulsion?"

"No. Do you recommend it?"

"Yes...but....You see, sir, it takes the interest out of it. I have begun sketching now, instead, to—" He broke off and shook his head. "Well, well. I didn't mean to discuss photography, or drawing, either, did I? Although my problem involves them both, in a manner of speaking."

"Yes?" said Holmes, placing his fingertips together.

"I wish to have a man found. He contracted with me to make zinc-blocks of *Alice's Adventures Under Ground*. That was the original title, you understand, on the manuscript. But now he has run off, and—"

Holmes's fingers fell between each other, leaving his hands clasped tightly together, and his chin jerked perceptibly. "You are Lewis Carroll, sir?"

"Certainly not." Then he looked discomfited and added, "He is my *nom de plume*. You will, of course, keep all this confidential?"

"Of course," said Holmes quickly.

"I have always had the greatest dread of being lionized, and so..." he trailed off.

"I quite understand," said Holmes, as if he sympathized, but his face fell at Mr. Dodgson's implicit refusal to listen to the panegyric he might have given on Lewis Carroll.

"Mr. Noad was recommended to me as an excellent photographer and engraver near Oxford, but one who was in so small a way of business that I should have to pre-pay him for the zinc-blocks. He did a set of negatives—first-rate, I may say—and delivered the blocks as he prepared them. I sent them on in turn to Mr. Macmillan.

There has been so much interest in *Alice* that he thought a facsimile edition of the manuscript would interest readers."

"It would," said Holmes.

"Suddenly in October Noad disappeared, with twenty-two of the blocks still undelivered. It is my belief that he is hiding from his creditors. Meanwhile, the original has gone back to...to the owner, Mrs. Hargreaves.[1] And it would be a p-pity to give her the trouble of lending it again, and risk losing it. Do you think you could find Mr. Noad—and the zinc-blocks?"

"Yes," said Holmes. "The human trail is one—"

But Mr. Dodgson nervously took his watch out of his waistcoat pocket and examined it. "Oh dear," he exclaimed, "I shall be too late." He hurried to the door. "Thank you, sir. If I decide to retain you, I shall return later this afternoon—if that is convenient?"

"Quite."

A few seconds later the front door opened and closed again, and to our surprise we heard Mr. Dodgson called into conversation at the doorstep.

"Why, Dodgson! Small world. What brings you to the metropolis?"

"M-my p-publisher." The other apparently made some gesture of amused incredulity, for Mr. Dodgson added, "And to consult a d-detective, M-mr. Sherlock Holmes."

Something about the coincidence of the meeting seemed to disturb Holmes and he edged around to peer out from the side of the open window. Imitating his caution, I did the same, and beheld another tall, thin gentleman. Like the scholar, he was marked with the look of attentiveness that bespeaks a keen intelligence, although marred in his case by a frown at once anxious and worldly.

"A detective? No serious trouble, I hope," said the stranger.

"Yes—that is, not p-precisely," said Mr. Dodgson, again consulting his watch. "I hoped he could locate Noad, the zincographer, you know. He absconded with my blocks."

"Hmmm. I shouldn't think so," said the stranger. "Confidentially, detectives are all more or less scoundrels. Comes of working too closely with the criminal classes."

"Surely not," said Mr. Dodgson, hesitantly.

"Fact. In any case, shouldn't you give your man a little longer? No doubt he'll return your goods when he's had time to...listen to

1. Mrs. Hargreaves: Mrs. Reginald Hargreaves, born Alice Liddell, The Alice of *Alice*.

his conscience. It's not as if he could get money for them elsewhere."

"Yes, p-perhaps....I don't suppose you know his whereabouts?"

"How should I?"

"Didn't he do some p-printing for you? I thought I saw your signature on some letters he was filing once."

"Oh, yes, I knew him slightly. But, there, I mustn't keep you, if you've an appointment. A pleasure to see you." He started to move on, then turned back, as if with a new idea. "Why don't you meet me after you leave Macmillan's, at my club? I've quite lost touch. Did you ever check out the Continental geometricians? You should, you really should."

"I meant to see Mr. Holmes again," said Dodgson, answering the first question. "But if you think the m-matter should wait...."

The stranger finished writing the address on a card and handed it over. "I'll see you later, then."

Holmes closed the window softly as the two parted, and he began to pace up and down the room. "More or less scoundrels!" he said. "And to Lewis Carroll!" He stopped and looked thoughtfully at the mirror. "Watson, I'll find that zincographer," he said.

For weeks thereafter he spent each weekend in Oxford, leaving by the first train and returning on the last, but his trips grew infrequent. In April the missing man called at Macmillan's, left a few of the blocks, and vanished. I congratulated Holmes, but he said it was none of his doing.

In the summer, however, Holmes located him in Eastbourne, living there under the name of Phillimore. He notified Mr. Dodgson, who had a warrant issued for the man's apprehension. But the wretched fellow begged to be given money, which he promised to repay later, to do the remaining blocks over. He did in fact finally deliver the blocks to Macmillan's, and made an appointment to see Mr. Dodgson to pay the debt.

He never kept the appointment.

He came out of his house, hailed a cab, observed that it was beginning to rain, went in again, and was never seen again.

The cabbie, I am told, was much annoyed.

Holmes again began devoting his weekends to the task of locating the zincographer, but without success. It was not till autumn when an investigation in Scandinavia drew him away from Oxford and Eastbourne that he gave up. The trail was cold, he said bitterly, and the game had gone to ground.

So in 1928 we were driven by motor through the rain, and there were neither hansoms nor horses to be seen on the London streets. I sighed, remembering Holmes's old disappointment. "What a pity you couldn't bring Lewis Carroll's Mr. Phillimore to justice."

To my surprise, Holmes began to laugh, drawing looks of disapproval from our fellow passengers. "Ah, but I think I did," he said. "Think back. *Who* told Lewis Carroll I was a scoundrel?"

"I don't know who he—" A vague memory stirred. I was seeing something that had nothing to do with Lewis Carroll. A crowd. What sort of a crowd, I asked myself. A crowd in a train station… Victoria station…and a man running for the train.…"Moriarty!"

"Just so, Watson."

"The zincographer was one of his men?"

"Obviously. Now, when Moriarty's gang was rounded up, there were only three among them who could have had a knowledge of zincography, his little band of counterfeiters. And you will remember that that were later proved to be the same who once employed your friend Victor Hatherly with such distressing results. How did you describe them?—the beautiful woman, the sinister German, and—"

"—the morose Englishman," I chimed in.

Holmes shook his head over the incurable romanticism of my epithets, but was too elated to comment on it. "And the Englishman was, therefore, James Phillimore. 'O frabjous day'!"[2] he said, and chortled in his joy.[3]

2. Those curious regarding Holmes's use of this Jabberwock expression should note a quotation attributed to Watson (though not literally) by Vincent Starrett, "O frabjous day! Callooh, Callay," in *The Private Life of Sherlock Holmes,* N.Y., 1933, p.47. –Ed.

3. The manuscript was sold in April 1928 to an American, A. S. W. Rosenbach of Philadelphia, who sold it to Eldridge R. Johnson of Moorestown, New Jersey, and bought it back after his death for $50,000. Luther H. Evans, then Librarian of Congress, thought *Alice* ought to be in England, persuaded Rosenbach to sell it, raised the money, and in 1948 gave it to the British Museum where it remains. (See *Alice's Adventures Under Ground,* a facsimile of the 1864 manuscript, introduction by Martin Gardner, New York, 1965.)

ARTHUR CONAN DOYLE (1859-1930):
MEDICAL AUTHOR
Jack D. Key

Note: Parts of the text are used with the kind permission of
Minnesota Medicine.

THE LITERARY WRITINGS of Arthur Conan Doyle can be recommended to all who are involved in the health sciences. His stories are liberally laced with references to matters of medical and scientific interest. As one reads through the adventures of Sherlock Holmes and Dr. Watson, as well as other Doyle masterpieces, it is obvious that the stories are written by a person well versed in medicine with its tenet of careful clinical observation. Something seems to be included for everyone, with many examples of contemporary British medical practices relating to anatomy, cardiology, chemistry, dermatology, forensic science, genetics, internal medicine, neurology, ophthalmology, otorhinolaryngology, pathology, pharmacology, physiology, psychiatry, surgery, toxicology, tropical medicine, and more. The medical references are neither trivial nor contrived but occur naturally in their places as commentaries on events as they happen— descriptions by a doctor as seen through his eyes.

My intent with this paper is to make a brief presentation of Doyle as a physician and to note his formal contributions to the medical literature.

Arthur Conan Doyle, creator[1] of Sherlock Holmes, was born in Edinburgh, Scotland, on May 22, 1859. His mother, concerned that he have a means of livelihood, advised Arthur to go to medical school. This he did after preliminary education at the Jesuit College at Stoneyhurst, Lancashire, England. Doyle graduated from the Edinburgh University in 1881 with the degrees of Bachelor of Medicine and Master of Surgery.

Contributing to his reservoir of experiences in these early years (much of which was subsequently incorporated into novels) were two brief sea voyages as ship's surgeon, first to the Arctic on a whaler and later to the west coast of Africa, and several short tours of duty as an assistant to doctors in England. Early in 1882 he

1. While Mr. Key is obviously well informed regarding the medical writings of Dr. Doyle, he seems unfamiliar with Dr. Doyle's activity as a "literary agent." —Ed.

became assistant to George Budd, an old medical school colleague, in Plymouth, England. This experience proved disappointing and shortly thereafter Doyle put up his own brass plate at Southsea. His practice during the next 8 years developed slowly—too slowly. Doyle then decided to become an eye specialist and in December 1890, he left for Vienna to study.

It is interesting to note at this point an excerpt from Doyle's *The Stark Munro Letters,* which is something of an autobiographical volume of his time spent with George Budd. In a conversation between Stark Munro (Doyle) and Cullingworth (Budd), the following comment appears:

> I've taken to the eye, my boy. There's a fortune in the eye. A man grudges a half-crown to cure his chest or his throat, but he'd spend his last dollar over his eye. There's money in ears, but the eye is a gold mine![2]

Another example of Doyle's thoughts on ophthalmology as a career appears in a letter he wrote to his sister. One also sees the hint of ambivalence concerning the financial role literature was soon to play in his destiny.

> If it *(Micah Clarke)* comes off, we may...have a few hundreds on hand to start us. I should go to London and study the eye. I should then go to Berlin and study the eye. I should then go to Paris and study the eye. Having learned all there is to know about the eye, I should come back to London and start as an eye-surgeon, still, of course, keeping literature as my milk-cow.[3]

Returning from the Continent in 1891, Doyle set up practice in London among the fashionable practitioners at Devonshire Place—but saw no patients.

Doyle at this time survived a severe bout of influenza and made up his mind to turn to full-time writing. Royalties from his books and checks for his short stories and other writings were pouring in. It was evident to him that what had started modestly with the sale of his first story in 1878 had subsequently, with many other publications, grown to an enjoyable and comfortable occupation. He would turn to medicine again only while treating British soldiers in

2. A. C. Doyle, *The Stark Munro Letters,* 2d ed., N.Y., D. Appleton and Co., 1895, p.379.

3. J. D. Carr, *The Life of Sir Arthur Conan Doyle,* N.Y., Harper & Brothers, 1949, p.54.

the Boer War in South Africa, a service for which he was knighted in 1902.

Altogether Dr. Doyle's medical activities covered a period of a little over 10 years. A career in medicine originally undertaken for practical purposes seemingly provided few of the hoped-for rewards. Perhaps the real answer to why Doyle did not make a greater impact on his chosen profession was that he lacked a genuine impetus toward medicine. In any case, Doyle's gift for literary writing emerged as his predominant activity.

One would think that Doyle, a born writer, might have contributed much to the formal literature of medicine. Circumstances, talent, and history were to dictate otherwse. In 1878, while he was yet a medical student, he wrote optimistically to his mother:

> Let me once get my footing in a good hospital and my game is clear. Observe cases minutely, improve in my profession, write to the *Lancet*, supplement my income by literature, make friends and conciliate everyone I meet, wait ten years if need be, and then when my chance comes be prompt and decisive in stepping into an honorary surgeonship.[4]

Doyle's first effort, "Gelseminum as a Poison," appeared in the September 20, 1879, issue (page 483) of the *British Medical Journal* as a letter to the editor. He described an experiment conducted on himself, his symptoms and his reactions to gradually increasing doses of gelseminum over a 7-day period.

His next contribution appeared in the March 25, 1882 issue (page 490) of *Lancet*. In this article, entitled "Notes on a Case of Leucocythaemia," Doyle suggested a connection between malaria and leukemia. There is little to mark it as being outstanding or anything other than just another case report. (The uncharitable finger of fate that can haunt any author recorded his name, misspelled, as A. Cowan Doyle instead of A. Conan Doyle.)

The third contribution, "The Remote Effects of Gout," published in *Lancet*, November 29, 1884, (pages 978-979), is another case report noting gout in three successive generations of the same family.

In 1885, after hard study at home, Doyle passed the examination and qualified for the M.D. degree, which was awarded to him by Edinburgh University. In partial fulfillment of the requirements for

4. P. Nordon, *Conan Doyle; A Biography*, N.Y., Holt, Rinehart and Winston, 1964, p.26.

this degree, an unpublished doctoral thesis was presented entitled "The Gouty Diathesis."

In 1890, after a trip to Berlin, Doyle published a letter of warning in the *Daily Telegraph* concluding that Robert Koch's tuberculin, being touted as a sure cure for consumption, was both experimental and premature.

While serving in the Boer War at the Langman Hospital in South Africa, Doyle responded to a suggestion from the editor of the *British Medical Journal* to submit notes on anything that might be of interest. He followed through on this suggestion with "The War in South Africa, The Epidemic of Enteric Fever at Bloemfontein," which appeared in the *British Medical Journal* 2:49-50, July 7, 1900. What he wrote was a vivid description of the toll taken by the disease and the courage, patience, and hard work displayed by those involved.

In *Lancet* 1:189, Jan. 19, 1907, and in the *British Medical Journal* 1:173, Jan. 19, 1907, Doyle, in letters to the editors, submitted a question for ophthalmologists concerning the case of George Edalji, who was found guilty of having mutilated a pony. In the cause of justice, Doyle sought a consensus of scientific opinion as to whether it was physically possible for Mr. Edalji, who had severe myopic astigmatism, to have committed this offense. Also in 1907 he wrote the foreword for *The Construction and Reconstruction of the Human Body*...by E. Sandow, published in London by John Bale, Sons & Co.

To the entering medical class at St. Mary's Hospital in 1910, Doyle presented an interesting talk titled "The Romance of Medicine." A recorder apparently transcribed this address, which appears in *Lancet* 2:1066-1068, 1910. Doyle's message was that training in medicine was both a valuable and a worthwhile background for any profession. He discussed the undue materialism of the period, warned against intellectual priggishness, and stressed the values of kindliness, humanity, and knowledge.

Doyle's final publication in the medical literature appears as an obituary for Captain Malcolm Leckie, D.S.O., R.A.M.C., in *Guy's Hospital Gazette* (London), v.29, pp.3-4, (Jan. 2, 1915). Leckie, formerly of Guy's Hospital, died of wounds on Aug. 28, 1914, at Frameries near Mons. He was attached to the Northumberland Fusiliers and had gone to the front with the Expeditionary Army.

Of Doyle's literary writings only *Round the Red Lamp, Being Facts and Fancies of Medical Life,* published in 1895, is of a medical nature. This work, a collection of short stories, is based on the common theme of a doctor's life. In these stories the author proved that his knowledge of medicine was based on more than hearsay and that he was acutely aware of the essential qualities of the good physician.

Conan Doyle was proud of the fact that he was a physician. In a letter to his mother he once mentioned "The title I value most is that of "Doctor," which was conferred by your self-sacrifice and determination."[5] Years later at a tea he hosted in July 1913 for Representatives of the Medical Association, Doyle observed that he "had the warmest feelings toward his old profession, and that the opportunity of renewing acquaintance with his old colleagues and entertaining them at tea was a source of great pleasure to him." He achieved eminence in another walk of life but was always willing to acknowledge generously his indebtedness to his former profession. At the same time, Doyle recognized that he had no possible claim to be regarded as a success in medicine. At the 1913 tea for Representatives of the Medical Profession, Doyle wryly recalled that once in America the chairman at a dinner at which he was present remarked that "it was a sinister fact that although Sir Arthur Conan Doyle was supposed to be a doctor no living patient of his had ever been seen."[6]

The ultimate loss to the medical profession as Doyle turned to writing full time is uncertain. The gain to literature was tremendous. A versatile Doyle firmly established himself in English literature not only with mysteries, crime, and detective fiction, but also with historical novels, short stories, volumes of poems, plays, histories, science fiction, and publications in occult science. He invented the most famous detective — Sherlock Holmes.[7] He enriched our lives. Conan Doyle — the man — died July 7, 1930; Conan Doyle — the author — lives on in the minds and hearts of multitudes. Appropriate is the epitaph that marks his grave: "Arthur Conan Doyle, Knight, Born May 22, 1859, Steel True, Blade Straight."

5. Carr, *op. cit.*, p.159.

6. "Sir Arthur Conan Doyle," *British Medical Journal*, v.2 (1913), p.192.

7. Mr. Key makes an interesting point here. Was Doyle actually the "inventor" who persuaded Watson to write up Holmes's adventures, and Holmes to permit them to be published? –Ed.

Arthur Conan Doyle's Medical writings Jack D. Key

"Gelseminum as a Poison." *British Medical Journal,* September 20, 1879, p.483.

"Notes on a Case of Leucocythaemia," *Lancet,* March 25, 1882, p.490.

"The Remote Effects of Gout," *Lancet,* November 29, 1884, pp.978-979.

"The Gouty Diathesis," Unpublished doctoral thesis, University of Edinburgh, 1885.

Letter of warning (regarding Robert Koch's tuberculin) *Daily Telegraph,* 1890.

"The War in South Africa, The Epidemic of Enteric Fever at Bloemfontein." *British Medical Journal,* v.2, pp.49-50, July 7, 1900.

Letter to the editor, *Lancet,* v.1, p.189, Jan. 19, 1907. (Question for ophthalmologists concerning George Edalji.)

Letter to the editor, *British Medical Journal,* v.1, p.173, Jan. 19, 1907.

Foreword for E. Sandow, *The Construction and Reconstruction of the Human Body.* London, John Bale, Sons & Co., 1907.

"The Romance of Medicine," transcribed address at St. Mary's Hospital, *Lancet,* v.2, pp.1066-1068, 1910.

Obituary for Captain Malcolm Leckie, D.S.O., R.A.M.C., *Guy's Hospital Gazette* (London) v.29, pp.3-4, Jan. 2, 1915.

Round the Red Lamp, Being Facts and Fancies of Medical Life. London, John Murray, 1895. (A collection of short stories of a medical nature.)

"Preface," *Alloquia; Experiences and some Reflections of a Medical Practitioner...* by D. Marinus. London, C. W. Daniel, 1928, pp.7-8.

A NOTE ABOUT CONTRIBUTORS

JOHN BENNETT SHAW. Certainly no Sherlockian needs another note about Mr. Shaw, B.S.I. (Unofficial Representative of Mr. Sherlock Holmes in the Country of the Garridebs). His bibliography is long and distinguished and he has probably attended more different Scion Society meetings than any other Sherlockian.

JOHN E. BERGQUIST is a store manager for Century Camera, Inc. of Minneapolis. A Holmes aficionado since junior high school, Mr. Bergquist marks his transition from fan to fanatic as the day he discovered William S. Baring-Gould's *The Annotated Sherlock Holmes*. It is regrettable that Mr. Bergquist did not get to know Mr. Baring-Gould while the latter was a student at the University of Minnesota.

RUTH BERMAN's Sherlockian writing has appeared in BSJ, *West by One and By One*, and in A Sherlockian Christmas Carol. She has also edited The SHsf Fanthology and contributed to science fiction collections. Of lesser importance to Sherlockians has been her contribution of poetry to literary magazines.

JOSEPH B. CONNORS is "in his spare time" Professor of English at the College of St. Thomas in St. Paul. On any test of Sherlockiana among the Norwegian Explorers he would certainly score high. It is suspected that Professor Connors was in part responsible for the installation of the Sherlock Holmes stained glass window in the Library of The College of St. Thomas, referred to in Mr. Shaw's delightful essay.

J. RANDOLPH COX, B.S.I. (The Conk-Singleton Forgery Case) Mr. Cox's writings should be well known to readers of the BSJ. In between his Sherlockian efforts he teaches detective and mystery literature (what else) at St. Olaf College, Northfield, and works in the St. Olaf College Library. In 1969 Mr. Cox taught a "new course in detective fiction" in which he was reputed to have dressed in his finest Sherlockian attire while teaching the class.

BRYCE L. CRAWFORD JR., though not yet a Nobel prize winner as were Explorers Dr. Philip S. Hench, and Dr. William Lipscomb, is one of the many distinguished chemists who have honored the Explorers with their membership. (Like Holmes who said "My collection of M's is a fine one," our Explorers' collection of chemists is likewise a fine one.) Dr. Crawford still resents the failure of the Explorers to reimburse him for the thirty-two cents cost of funicular transportation in Meiringen in 1957, a "story for which the world is not clamoring."

RONALD M. HUBBS, recently Chairman of the Board, and former President of the St. Paul Companies, Inc., divides his retirement time between the activities of the Norwegian Explorers and the tremendous number of business, cultural, and philanthropic Boards of Trustees of which he is a member. Mr. Hubbs richly exemplifies those important qualifications of a business entrepreneur which he discusses in "Holmes: The Potential Entrepreneur."

JACK D. KEY, Librarian of the Mayo Clinic and Assistant Professor of Biomedical Communications, Mayo Medical School, Rochester, Minnesota, has written extensively for professional journals in medicine as well as librarianship and library automation. His article, we believe, is the first attempt to discover and identify the medical writings of the "literary agent."

E. W. MCDIARMID, B.S.I. (Bruce-Partington Plans) is the Sigerson of the Norwegian Explorers and Professor emeritus of the Library School, University of Minnesota. Although he grew up in Texas he has managed to survive the colder climate of the "Land of the Sky Blue Water." To date his travels have not been as extensive nor as imaginative as those of the "real" Sigerson as reported in the Sacred Writings.

Sumac Press

EMERSON G. WULLING

613 North 22 Street   La Crosse, Wis. 54601